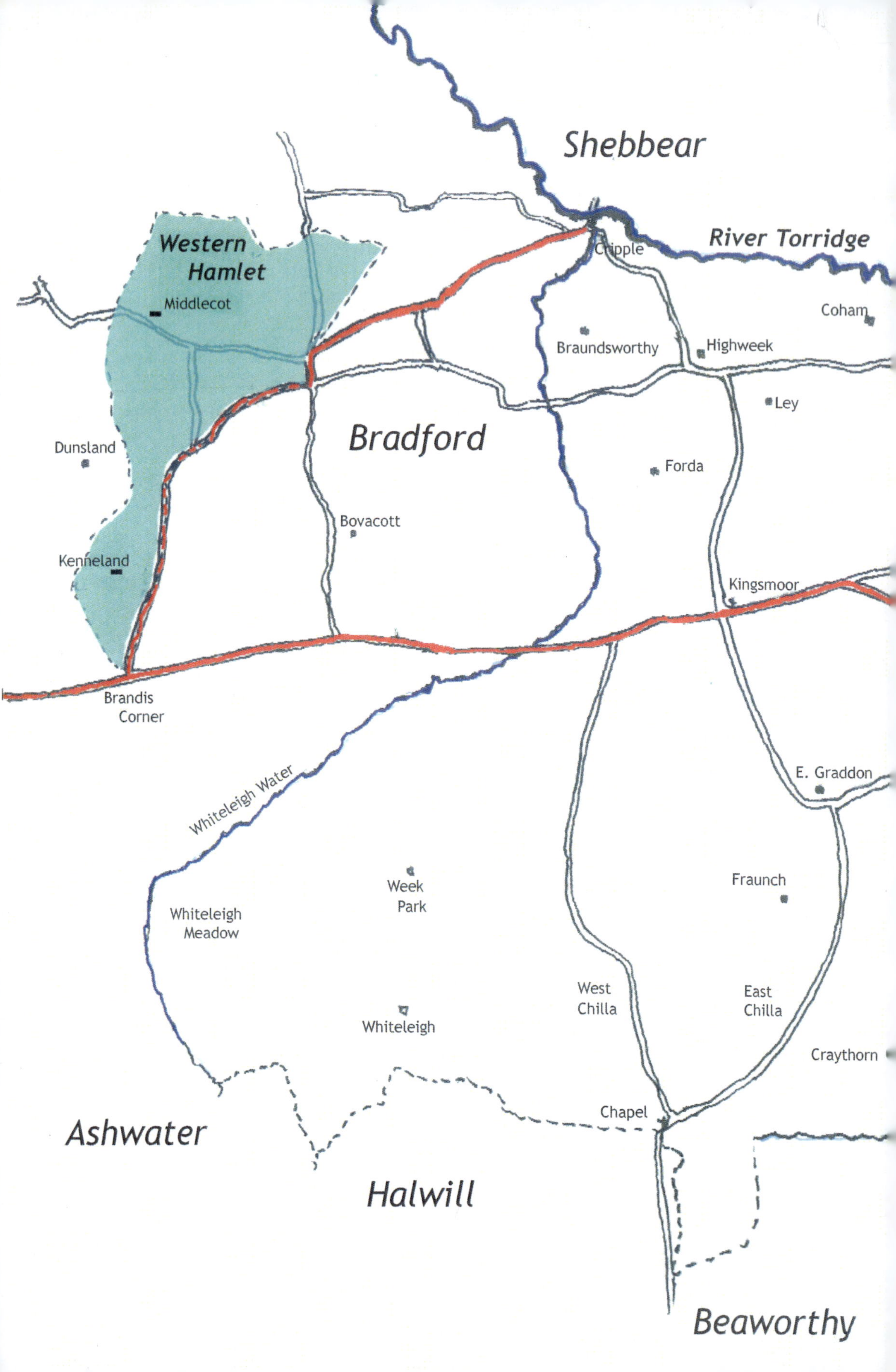
Shebbear
River Torridge
Western
Hamlet
Middlecot
Cripple
Coham
Braundsworthy
Highweek
Ley
Dunsland
Bradford
Forda
Bovacott
Kenneland
Kingsmoor
Brandis
Corner
E. Graddon
Whiteleigh Water
Fraunch
Week
Park
Whiteleigh
Meadow
West
Chilla
East
Chilla
Whiteleigh
Craythorn
Chapel
Ashwater
Halwill
Beaworthy

Sheepwash
Eastern Hamlet
Totleigh
Ditsham
East Totleigh
Keyethern
Mill
Church
Bridge
Kneela
Buckpitt
Smithsland
Chapel
Hayne
Butterbeare
Upcott
Beara
Highampton
S. Trew
Hole
Burdon
Wagaford Water
Northlew
Scale 1 Mile

BLACK TORRINGTON
THE SECOND MILLENNIUM

Gerry Matthews

Edward Gaskell
DEVON

Edward Gaskell *publishers*
Old Gazette Building
6 Grenville Street
Bideford
Devon
EX39 2EA

isbn 1-898546-61-4
First published 2003
This edition 2011
©Gerry Matthews

BLACK TORRINGTON
THE SECOND MILLENNIUM

Gerry Matthews

This book is sold subject to the condition that it shall not be re-sold, lent, hired out or otherwise circulated in any binding or cover other than that in which it is published and without a similar condition being imposed upon the subsequent purchaser without the express consent of the publishers.

Typeset, Printed and Bound by
Lazarus Press
Unit 7 Caddsdown Business Park
Bideford
Devon
EX39 3DX
www.lazaruspress.com

To Katharine
a child of the village

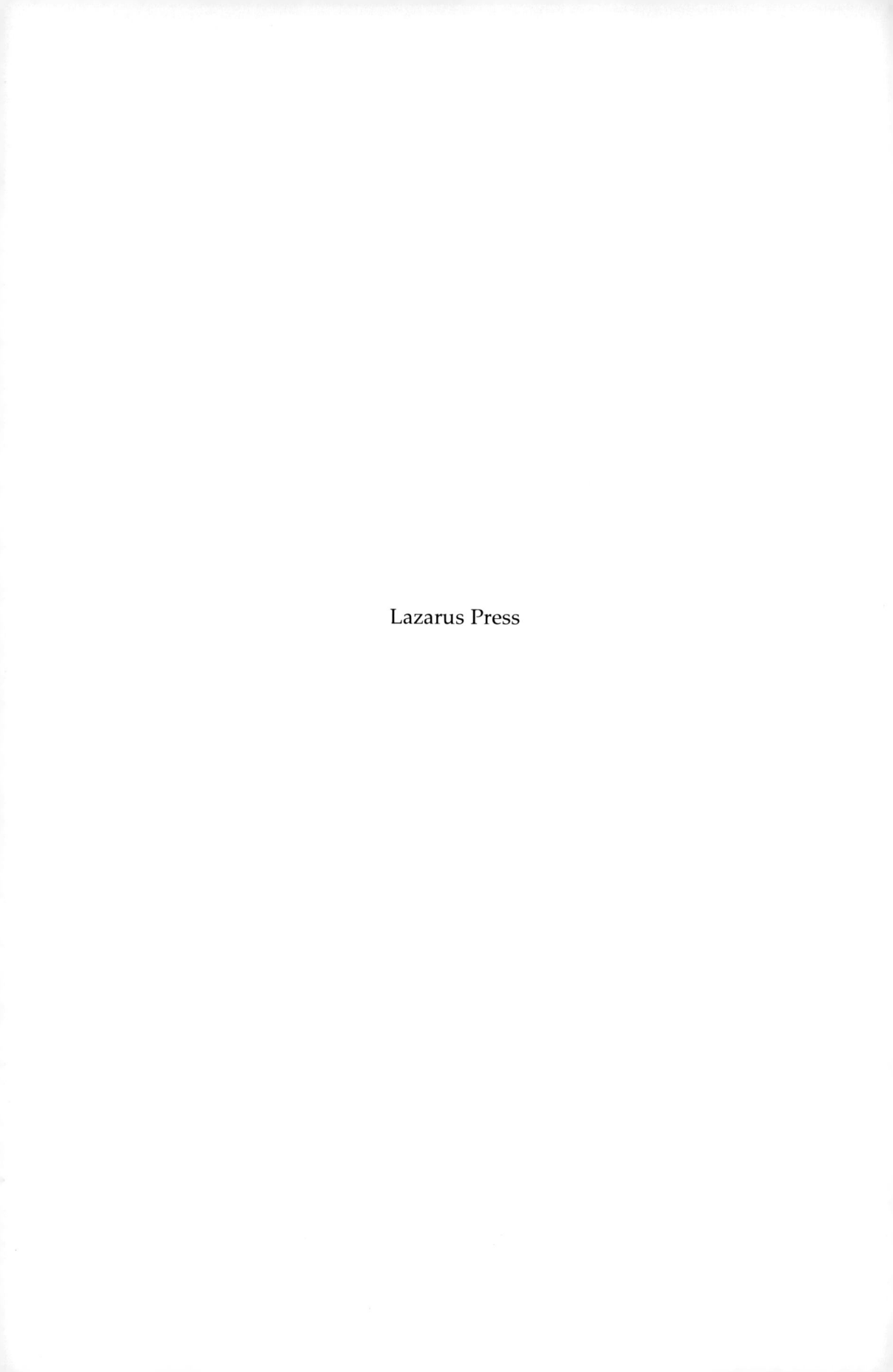

Lazarus Press

The Author

Gerald Matthews was born in Bridgwater, Somerset in 1931, and moved at an early age to Bridport in Dorset. He was educated at West Buckland School in North Devon, where he spent seven years, and Bristol University, where he read law and was a member of the Bristol University Dramatic Society.

After two years' National Service with the Royal Signals Regiment he studied for ordination at Ripon Hall, Oxford and was made deacon by the Bishop of Birmingham in 1957.

He returned to the West Country as Vicar of Brent Tor in 1963 and in 1978 became Priest-in-Charge of Black Torrington, where he has remained, retiring from stipendiary ministry in 1990.

His interests include history, drama, collecting (and reading) books.

CONTENTS

Introduction	9
Early History	13
The Norman Conquest	15
Medieval Times	17
The Church	21
16th Century Families	27
The Stuarts and The Civil War	33
The Restoration and The Eighteenth Century	37
The Nineteenth Century	45
The Lords of the Manor	53
The Village Inns	57
Doctors	61
Schools	65
Crime and the Police	75
The Church 1790–2000	79
Chapels	97
Charities	101
Parish Council	103
The Public Hall	115
The Playing Field	121
War Times	129
Sports and Pastimes	133
Decline of Trade and Shops	139
Into the Future	147
Appendices	149
Index	157

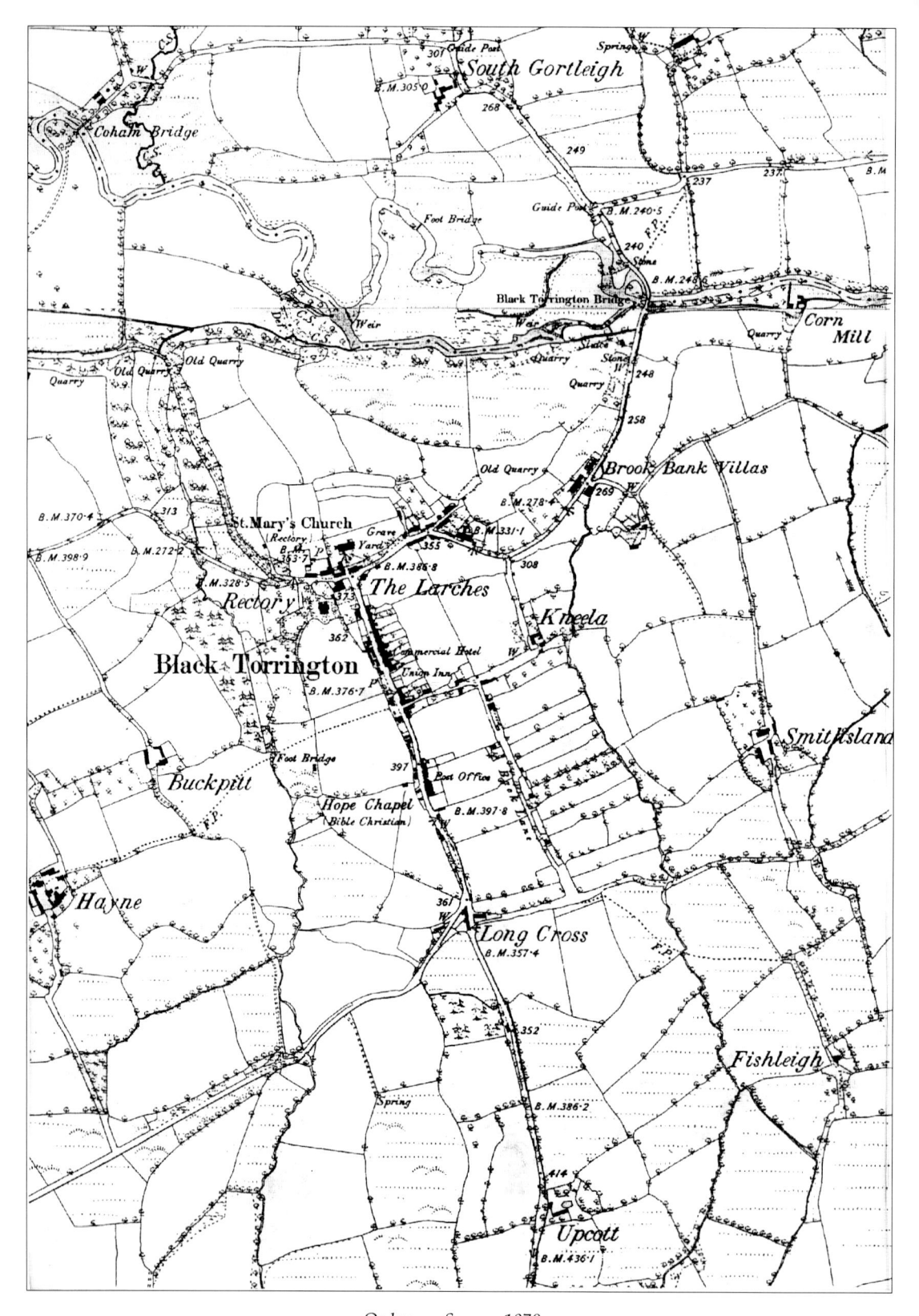

Ordnance Survey 1870

INTRODUCTION

Black Torrington is a small village, in a parish that covers over eight square miles, some ten miles north west of Okehampton and eight miles east of Holsworthy. The parish church stands at 385 feet above sea level. It was in existence before the Norman Conquest and gave its name to one of the Saxon administrative areas known as 'hundreds'.

As the second millennium of our present calendar was drawing to a close it seemed an appropriate moment to try to sketch a thousand years of local history. Time has overtaken the process of gathering, sorting and setting down the discoverable facts and it has taken an additional year to get them ready for publication.

Norman and Mediaeval records are few, as might be expected; from the Tudor ages onwards they become increasingly available, until the twentieth century when the amount can be overwhelming.

I hope I have been able to get the balance right. When writing about events within living memory I am conscious of the ease with which it is possible to offend, both by omission and inclusion. I have tried to ensure that nothing is included which is not already in some way on public record.

I am indebted to many who have been sources of information: from past to present historians – principally Sir William Pole in the 16th century, Tristram Risdon, Thomas Westcote, John Prince and Richard Polwhele in the 17th century, Daniel Lysons in the 19th century and W.G.Hoskins in the 20th. In the late 19th and early 20th century the Revd. J.R. Powell of Buckland Filleigh contributed regular articles to the local press and left volumes of manuscript notes about local families and ancient customs. The earliest official record in England is the so-called 'doomsday book' of 1086. A translation of the Devonshire Domesday was published by the Devonshire Association in 1884 edited by J.Brooking Rowe. The Revd. Oswald Reichel (brother of L.H.Reichel of Black Torrington) did much work on this and on the Hundreds of Devon for the Association between 1894–1922. From the Middle Ages to the 20th century there are many statistical returns of tax, property and census that have been made available by the Devon Records Office and the West Country Studies Library in Exeter. There are also Diocesan, parish and parish council records and many newspapers, in particular the *Exeter Flying Post*, the *Western*

Times, the *Western Morning News* and the *Holsworthy Post*. Many local people have supplied valuable information of their family histories and the part they played in more recent events. The tithe survey undertaken in 1842 records every owner and every tenant of every property in the parish. In addition the county directories, published by White in 1850 and 1878, by Billings in 1857 and by Kelly, intermittently from 1856-1939, are a great source of information.

A word of explanation is necessary about early names and dates. Before the 18th century the spelling of proper names was not standardized; one could even say that spelling generally was not standardized. In the text I have often given the names of places and people as they appeared in the documents of the time and therefore there is some inconsistency. Recording dates before 1752 requires some care. In that year the calendar reckoning altered. In the old Julian calendar the year began on 25th March, therefore in the years before 1752 dating for January-March can be confusing, and so any date in that period for the earlier years is given a double figure – e.g. 14th March 1677/8 – to remind the reader that the relevant dates given as 1677 are, to our way of thinking, 1678.

Coinage has also changed over the centuries. The mark, which went out of use in the 15th century, was worth 13s.4d. There is a more recent change as £.s.d. (pounds, shillings and pence) changed to £.p. (pounds and pence) with decimalization in 1971. Thus the medieval mark (13s.4d.) would be approximately 67p. I have sometimes given modern equivalents, but of course the value of money has changed enormously. In the thousand years of this past millennium the value of money has declined by a factor of 90 or more. The mark of the 15th century would now be of the value of about £43. £1 at the time of the Armada (1588) would now be worth about £55, and £1 in 1800 would in the year 2000 be worth about £48. These calculations must be very approximate especially as the value that man puts upon things varies with the centuries.

The probate of wills is another source of information. Unfortunately Devon suffered a great loss in the blitz of Exeter in 1942 when incendiary bombs destroyed part of the central library archive and all the deposit of Devon wills. All was not lost however as some had been transcribed by two recorders and these transcripts are preserved, but they only comprise a few of the total. Further sources of information are in the records of the civil, ecclesiastical and criminal courts. Most of these are not indexed and to find reference to an individual in a small parish in Devonshire is much like looking for a needle in a haystack.

Finally there are legends, traditions and local folklore. These need testing and tracing as they are often transferred from one person or one place to another, but they can contain items of interesting history. I have been particularly helped by the memories of the late Leslie Ivey, of Ralph Chapman and Brian Down.

Wistaria on The Rectory stables, 1959, before conversion to a dwelling

The illustrations are mainly from picture postcards published from about 1900 onwards and some collected photographs. There were living in Black Torrington in the 1970s and '80s two very accomplished amateur photographers, R.K. Battson and A.J. Butler, and some of their work is included. A number have been lent, in particular by Mrs Stella Maynard (née Broad), Mrs Jacqueline Sleeman (née Dart), Mr Ernest Luxton, Mr William Coham-Fleming and Mr Maurice Thomas. The manuscript has also benefited from the memoirs of the late Mrs Laura Luxton.

I have been encouraged in this work by Ernest Martin, a long time resident of Black Torrington and himself a social historian and university lecturer: also by Professor Nicholas Orme of Exeter University, who told me that professional historians rarely have the time or means to research local history and that this is often only to be done by the dedicated amateur, among whom the clergy hold a very good record!

Gerry Matthews
The Larches, Black Torrington, May 2002.

Black Torrington Bridge spanning the River Torridge, the parish boundary with Sheepwash.

EARLY HISTORY

The beginning of the second millennium makes a good starting point for a history of Black Torrington as there is little that can be discovered about events concerning the parish in the first millennium. However it will be helpful to summarize some of the earlier historical facts of the surrounding district. We know that in pre-historic times there were Bronze Age (1700-1000 B.C.) settlements on Dartmoor and on some other high moorland. Bronze Age barrows have been identified in Putford, and those barrows or tumuli in Beaworthy and Halwill may also be of that period. There were Iron Age settlements (900-100 B.C.) around the edge of Dartmoor. Clovelly Dykes are perhaps the nearest evidence of Iron Age occupation together with the fortifications of Brent Tor. The Romans we know moved westward from Exeter (Isca) in the second half of the first century A.D. There was a Roman fort at Okehampton, and there is evidence of some Roman occupation in a few place names such as Scobchester in Ashbury. Broadbury Down was also thought to be a place of Roman encampment.

The Celtic occupation of Devon was sparse, but enough to attract the Celtic Christian missionaries from Brittany, Ireland and Wales who sailed to the coasts of Devon and Cornwall in the fifth, sixth and seventh centuries. The earliest of these was the Breton, St Germanus (later bishop of the Isle of Man), who possibly founded the church at Germansweek and died circa 474. The most famous was the Welsh St Petrock who landed at Padstow and travelled widely in Devon and Cornwall: Newton St Petrock and Petrockstow indicate his presence in this area. He died at Bodmin in 594. By the end of this period the Saxons were making their peaceful invasion from the East. Near Henscott in Bradford there is an old fortified camp in Castle Wood overlooking the river Torridge. Tradition had it that these earthworks go back to the time of Hengist in the 5th century but there is no evidence to support this theory. The late Percy Russell, F.S.A., suggested that Totleigh in nearby Highampton preserves a Saxon name – "Tota's clearing".

By the eighth century, perhaps a little earlier, the settlement of Black Torrington must have been in existence. The formation of administrative and judicial districts, called 'hundreds', took place in the reign of Edmund (grandson of Alfred the Great) circa 940 A.D., and **Torintona** (Torrington) was the name given to the Hundred, of 35 parishes, which stretched from Bradworthy, in the west, to Sampford Courtenay, in the east. (Great Torrington was in the Hundred of Fremington, and Little Torrington was in the Shebbear Hundred). Black Torrington was the Hundred Manor, and was held before the Norman Conquest (1066) by the earl Harold. The outlier of the manor (a sub-manor) was **Mildelcota** (Middlecot) held by Alwold.

Venn c. 1976. The last village cottage to keep its thatch.

THE NORMAN CONQUEST

The Domesday Book of 1086 was a survey of the lands of England by officials sent to every county to obtain information from each village or manor in order to make a record of the King's rights and income from tax or rents. Black Torrington is recorded as a royal manor of 2680 acres worth £18. It included Totleigh (now in Highampton), Northcot and Whitleigh (in Chilla), East Wanford in Milton Damerel and South Wanford in Thornbury as well as East Kimber in Northlew and Kenland in Middlecot (now in Bradford). Middlecot itself, an outlier of Black Torrington, was a separate manor in the possession of Ranulf held from Baldwin de Brion the Sheriff of Devon. Baldwin, the son-in-law of William the Conqueror, was given the barony of Okehampton after the conquest and held 181 manors in Devon (164 held by under-tenants) including Bradford and its two sub-manors, Dunsland and Lashbrook.

The King held in possession in the manor of Torintona two virgates (a virgate = 30 acres) and land for six ploughs (a plough = a team of 8 oxen). The villeins (tenant farmers) had five virgates and 25 ploughs. There were 20 villeins, 22 bordars (cottagers with a little land), 10 swineherds and 15 serfs (slaves with no land). There were recorded 78 head of cattle, 30 swine, 200 sheep and 50 goats. There were 20 acres of meadow, three square miles (1920 acres) of pasture and a half square mile of wood (the other 420 acres must have been regarded as waste – moor, heath or marsh).

The first recorded designation of 'Black' for Torrington is in the Pipe Rolls (Exchequer records) of 1167 where it appears as '**Blacktoriton**'. There has been some conjecture about the name 'Black'. There was an idea that it might have come from the Saxon lord, Edmar the Black. However the Edmar who held Torintona at the death of Edward the Confessor was not 'the Black' and the Torintona in question was not in fact Black Torrington but one of the other Torringtons. Another theory was that it was 'Blake's Torrington' because of a spelling in the Pipe Roll of 1210 and the Fees Roll of 1219 which read '**Blake torrinton**', but 'Blake' has not been identified as a person. Thomas Westcote completed his *View of Devonshire* about 1630 in which he writes, "Black Torrington took his forename of the soil of the river." The bed of the river

Torridge which forms the northern boundary of the parish has many black stones along this part of its course. This seems the most acceptable reason for the name.

There is much evidence of Norman building in several churches in the neighbourhood – Bradford, Highampton and Shebbear to name but three.

Totleigh Barton

MEDIEVAL TIMES

The first local place name to be recorded is '**Cuham**' in the Pipe Rolls of 1230 in the reign of Henry II. This is the Saxon 'cow-ham', and gave its name to the family who lived there, and has continued to live there, perhaps for the whole of the second millennium – Coham. One hundred years before this, in the reign of Henry I, the king exchanged the hundred manor of 'Blaketoriton' for lands in France and elsewhere, giving Black Torrington to an ancestor of Joel de Mayne (or Johel de Meduana) a Norman. During the 12th century Joel, while retaining the manor, made over the Hundred and the liberties, including Wanford, Whiteleigh and Northcot, for a yearly payment of one mark (13s.4d. or 67p.) to Richard son of Esbus. Joel forfeited the manor for taking part in a rebellion and King John gave the lands to Geoffrey (or Galfrid) de Luci to hold as bailiff.

In 1227 Henry III granted the 'manor of Blacktorington, with Toteleigh its lordship' to Roger la Zouche (or de la Soche), who gave it to William la Zouche, his younger son, who dwelt at Toteleigh. Roger la Zouche was Sheriff of Devon in 1227 and '28 and again in 1230. In each instance Ralph Clark acted for him. Through William it descended to Alan la Zouche, who was also lord of North Molton, in 1241. The Zouches also held **Merland** (Little Marland) in Petrockstow. Alan gave Black Torrington to his younger son, William, who held it in 1275. In 1278 Henry Fitzwarren (the earliest recorded Rector of the parish) was presented as chaplain to 'Blake Torintone' church by Sir Roger la Zouche who held the advowson (the right to present to the ecclesiastical living of a parish).

In 1314 Sir Alan la Zouche, of Ashby and North Molton, held the advowson when he died. At this date the manor was held by Almeric (or Emery) la Zouche, son of William, who was born at Toteley in 1268. Sir William Pole (writing circa 1590) says that the daughter of Almeric la Zouche married Walter Fitzwarren and that their son, Almarick, who was sheriff of Devon in 1348–1350 and 1362, is recorded as having been lord of Black Torrington in the Inquisition of Henry V in 1420. At that date the lordship passed to his cousin William Davylles who was 30 years of age. William was the son of Isabel

Fitzwarren who married Thomas Davils of Badeston (in the parish of Malborough near Kingsbridge).

In addition to the manorial rights there were the rights, liberties (privileges) and possession of the <u>Hundred</u> of Black Torrington. These were granted to Richard de Wanford before 1199 and were inherited by his son, Thomas de Wanford (or Waumford), who held them in 1274. The family was seated at Whiteley where there was a caracate (or hide) of land which was 30 acres (considered to be as much land as one team of oxen could plough in a year). The heir of Eustace de Wanford was taxed by Edward I in 1302 at one half fee. The family continued there for the best part of another century until the death of Nicholas de Wanford when it passed, through his daughter Joan, to John Keines who held it in 1420 (John Keynes was Sheriff of Devon in 1399). His granddaughter married John Speake, of Bramford Speke, who sold the Hundred lordship to Hurst of Exeter. Richard Polwhele in his History of Devonshire, written about 1800, states that the Lordship was inherited by Sir Nicholas Martin, knight, in the early 17th century. In a manuscript History of Hatherleigh, written by J.S.Short circa 1830, it is stated that the Court Baron for the Hundred of Black Torrington was held in the early 19th century at the George Inn, Hatherleigh. It gives details of four Courts held between 1727-41 including one held at Clawton Bridge on 23rd June 1737, when the Steward was Charles Burdon and the Lord of the Hundred was William Clifford Martyn Esq. of Kenton, who died in 1769. The Court was concerned about a "bright bay nagg" which was a stray. As it was unclaimed a year later it was forfeited to the Lord of the Hundred. In 1810 the lordship was held by John Gullett, of Exeter, but by 1822 it was held by George Martyn Young of Nether Exe, a descendant of William Martin.

In the thirteenth and fourteenth centuries a number of place names in Black Torrington were recorded. **Childeton** (Chilla) appears as early as 1236: in the Subsidy Roll of 1330 it appears as **Chille**. **Brendesworth** (Braunsworthy) is mentioned in the Assize Rolls of 1238, **Gratedon** (Graddon), **Triwe** (Trew) and **Wagheford** (Wanford) in 1244, **Kingesmore** in 1249 and **Uppecote** in 1270. In the Assize Roll of 1304 we can find **la Knylle** (Kneela) and **Boterbeare** (Butterbear). **Whiteleye** is named in the Calendar of Inquisitions in 1307. **Crowethorne** (Craythorne in Chilla) appears in the Exeter Episcopal register of 1311, and **Bukapitte** (Buckpitt) in 1313. In the 1330s Subsidy Rolls for taxation we find the names of several people with the place of their abode: Nicholas atte **Beare** (Beara), William atte **Hole**, Adam atte **Forde** (Forda), Henry atte **Heghen** (Hayne) and John atte **Leye**. **Cromhale** is recorded in the Subsidy Roll of 1333. Cromhale means a crook in the river; this later changes to Crimple and then, by 1744, to Cripple and may be identified as the last dwelling in the parish in the north west near to Dipper Mill in Shebbear, now the Old Forge. (William Balsdon had a blacksmith's shop there until the 1940s).

The Zouches and the Fitzwarrens lived at the manor house of Toteley, in fact a sub-manor of Black Torrington, an outlier in what is now the parish of Highampton and on the site of the present Totleigh Barton. The house is reputed to have been moated and to have possessed fishponds; and there is a tale that King John himself came to enjoy the hunting there as a guest of the Lucy family in the early 13th century. We know the house had a chapel because an oratory licence was granted in 1401 to Dame Thomasine, widow of Sir Walter Fitzwarren, and to Almeric Fitzwarren Esq. and Margaret his wife, for 'the chapel of St Catherine the Virgin at Toteley'. Almeric Fitzwarren was Sheriff of Devon from 1348-50 (during the time of the Black Death) and again in 1362. In 1464 a man named Hozer bequeathed in his will 'to the Keeper of the Chapel of St Catherine the Virgin in Black Torrington, one missal, a set of vestments and also one altar cover and one chalice'. There is today a farm near East Totleigh called Keyethern (or Keyetherine) which is no doubt in some way linked to this chapel.

In the Lay Subsidy list for Devon in 1332 (compiled for the purpose of taxation) Thomas de Waunford heads the list with a charge of two shillings (10p). Among those charged at one shilling were Almeric fitz Waryn and William le Zouche. Walter de **Couham** (Coham) was assessed at ten pence (4p), as also was Michael **Bokkeberd** (another early reference to Butterbear). Several names refer to the detached western part of the parish – among the higher payers was Henry de **Middelcote** (1/-) and, at 8d., John de **Kynalonde** (Kenneland).

The successors of the Fitzwarrens were the Davylles, who had already become possessed of Merland in Petrockstow by marriage to the heiress of Zouche. Johane, wife of Thomas Davyle, was cited in a letter of attorney in 1452 as having possession of lands in north and south Wanford, Whytelaye (Whiteleigh) and Weekparke. Though the family lived mostly at Merland (Marland) they also resided at Toteleigh. John Davyls was in possession of Black Torrington mill in 1521 and 'two grist mills and one fulling mill in Tottley and Black Torrington' in 1565. John, the son of John Davells was baptized at Black Torrington in 1568, and Winifrede Davells married John Parsons, an attorney, at Black Torrington in 1576. The manor passed again by marriage during the reign of Elizabeth I, when Margaret the sole heiress of John Davylles married Arthur Harris of Hayne in the parish of Stowford. The lordship remained with the Harris family until the 19th century.

Looking north down Broad Street, c. 1890. The church is centre picture. Pellews Cottages on the right.

THE CHURCH

There may have been a Saxon church in Black Torrington, but we do not know. Or even a Celtic church, for the Celtic missionaries certainly came into Devon from Cornwall in the 6th century; but such a building would have been of mud, wood and thatch and no evidence of one has been found. The nearest recorded pre-Conquest church was at Hatherleigh. During the restoration of the present building in 1900 a stone with Norman carving was found built into the wall, which was then thought to date from about 1100. It has now been set over the piscina in the north transept. There was also found a carved head of early date that is now set in the south porch. Many of the local churches have Norman remains still existing. There is an old legend of uncertain date, similar to ones appertaining to many churches in the West Country, that the devil interfered with the building of the church. It was said that after the stones were collected by day,

The Church before restoration c.1890. Note the encaustic tiles in the chancel, the box pews, and the brass corunnas for candlelight.

the next morning the devil had spirited them away to Highweek, some mile or so to the west. Whether the fact that there is a field at Highweek called 'churchyard' has anything to do with this legend is a matter of conjecture. Nor do we have any evidence as to whether there was a Saxon church before the Norman one, but it was said that in the early part of the 19th century there were found in the field above the churchyard the foundations of an old building. These were apparently dug up and used to rebuild Church House in Broad Street (next to the bus shelter) in the 19th century.

In 1901 the roof of the nave was replaced. That which preceded it was said to have been a 14th century construction and was dated as 1370. Evidence for this precise date has not been preserved and it is more probable that it was contemporary with the granite piers of the arcade which are likely to be not earlier than 15th century. The 13th century church was probably cruciform in shape – chancel in the east, north and south transepts and nave running westwards, with no tower. If the granite arcades are mid 15th century then the south transept would have become part of the present south aisle. The tower was probably built around 1500. The period from 1440–1540 was a great age of church building and re-building in Devon, and many towers are dated in this period. The octagonal granite font also dates from the perpendicular style of the 15th century. The south porch, the windows of the south aisle and the aisle's wagon roof all date from about 1500. Who the benefactors were who donated the first building and its enlargement we do not know. Further building or restoration was probably completed in 1588/9, seven months after the defeat of the Armada, which is indicated by a stone inserted in the east wall of the church on which is inscribed 'Febr 26 1588. G. Closse.' This stone was reset when the chancel was re-built in 1902. The dedication to St Mary is not known to be recorded before 1742.

Although we know the names of the 14th century rectors, details of them are scant; some stayed but a short time and several had dispensations for non-residence for the purpose of study. Presumably these were young men. The first of them, Robert Pollard, was made deacon in December 1308, and had a dispensation for non-residence in order to study from 1st May 1309 until Michaelmas. The next was Elias de Tyngwyke in February 1313/4, who was only a sub-deacon! He again was granted non-residence for one year from May. Possibly he never came back, for in September 1315 Walter de Cromhale, priest, was instituted. The patronage (right to appoint) had by this time passed from Sir Alan la Zouche to Sir Nicholas de St Maur (his son-in-law who had married Helen de la Zouche). Walter also was granted one year's non-residence to study from September 1516, which was renewed the following year on condition that he put out his benefice to farm for two years, and "shall give to the fabric of the cathedral of Exeter 40 shillings" (£2). In 1317 a writ was issued against him and one other for wrongfully taking goods and chattels from Osney Abbey, near Oxford, to the value of 100 shillings.

Soon after this Bishop Stapledon held an ordination in the parish church of Black Torrington, on the Feast of St Andrew, 30th November 1319. Eleven men were ordained to the priesthood. Whether one of them was to serve Black Torrington we do not know. What else brought him to Black Torrington? He did of course have a brother, Sir Richard, living at Stapledon in Cookbury at that time. The next name to appear in the records is in 1331 when William, Rector of Black Torrington, a monk of Tavistock Abbey, is given leave of non-residence for one year. The next institution is of John de Wike, priest, who was presented in June 1344 by Sir Alan de Cherleton (Sir Alan had married the widow of Nicholas St Maur). Eleven years later Sir Alan presented his kinsman Griffin de Cherleton, who resigned after only two years. His successor, Thomas de Byschebury, likewise served only two years and may not have taken up residence at all. There is a mention of his proxy, William Payn, who was cited in a claim in May 1359 where he is described as chaplain of Black Torrington. In that year William Poltone was instituted, and two years later yet another Rector, William Falewille. The patron was now the son and heir of Sir Nicholas St Maur (or Seymor) as Lady Helen Cherleton had died, but, as he was a minor, patronage was exercised by the King (Edward III). Although Falewille was instituted in October 1361, he was not priested until April 1362, when he was ordained by the Bishop of Winchester in Farnham Castle, on Letters Dimissory from the Bishop of Exeter. A William Falewille became Rector of Ermington in South Devon in 1363. Whether he is the same William, and whether he held the two livings in plurality, we do not know. The next institution in the records is of Thomas de Sekyndone in 1370, also presented by the king. Thomas had leave for non-residence for at least four years between 1370-75 and in 1380 he exchanged benefices with Simon de Morecote from Bletchingly in Sussex.

By then the patron was Sir Richard Seymour, lord of Castle Cary, and he continued to hold the advowson until the end of the century. In 1390 he presented John Wyndout, another monk from Tavistock, who was made Penitentiary to receive confessions of the clergy of the Deanery of Holsworthy. In 1405 he exchanged livings with David Lovering, the Rector of St Mary Steps in Exeter. David Lovering was presented by Ela, the widow of Sir Richard Seymour, and David had "licence to celebrate on the Feast of her nativity in the Chapel of the Blessed Virgin Mary at Whiteley". This was probably for John Keynes. In 1430 the king (Henry VI) exercised the patronage in favour of Robert Wyot who resigned within six months and was followed by William Estby. On his death John Coke, alias White, was instituted in 1437 when the patron was John de St Maur Esq. In 1459 the last St Maur name occurs – Sir Thomas – who presented John Webber on the resignation of Thomas Faulkener. In the year 1463 Sir William Bampfield of Poltimore married Margaret the heiress of John Lord St Maure and by this union the Bampfylde family came to hold the advowson until the 19th century.

Agreement by local landowners to the tithe commutation in 1843

George Paige
Joseph Chapman
Mary Heysett
Richard Balsdon
Holland Coham
Thomas Snell

John Penleaze
Lewis R Heysett
Lewis W Buck (signed on behalf of)
William Chapman

...ment bearing date on or about the fifteenth day of
... and forty one the Tithes of the Parish of Black
... the Rent Charge in the said Agreement specified but no
Now it is hereby agreed by and between the
... Parish by whom or by whose Agents duly authorized
... in the said Rent Charge and Lands of the said
... nding Parochial Agreement under the Statutes for the
... Rent Charge shall commence and begin to run from
... whereof the Parties to this Agreement by themselves
... their names and affixed their seals this thirtieth day
... dred and forty three.

Elizabeth Burdon (signed on behalf of)   John Sanders
Charles Burdon   Arscott Venton
Richard Stenlake (mark X of)
Ezekiel Leach
Elias Leach

The Revd. William Bickford Coham 1793–1843

16th CENTURY FAMILIES

In 1538 Henry VIII ordered that registers of baptisms, marriages and burials be kept in every parish. The Black Torrington register begins in 1545 with the baptism of Katherine, the daughter of Thomas Hayne. The first marriage recorded is between John Pawlinge and Elizabeth Glawen in 1547, and the first burial is that of John Hurde in 1548. The first extensive list of names for the parish is the Subsidy Roll of 1525, which was compiled for tax purposes during the war against France. In Black Torrington the landowners who were taxed were Thomas Stevens and Thomas Wytte. Those who were substantially taxed on their goods (or wealth) were Nicholas Burdon and Thomas Nucombe, followed by Edmund Burdon, John Coham and Nicholas Thorne. **Brond** (Braund) and **Stemelake** (Stenlake) were other prominent names. Alice, the wife of John Coham, was buried in 1552. John appears to have had three sons, Thomas, Stephen and Christopher, but unfortunately many of the family records were lost when Coham House suffered a severe fire about the year 1700. Stephen Coham married Margaret Heysed in February 1567/8, and is the progenitor of the present family.

The Rectory before the 20th century extension

John Denis Burdon 1769–1842.

In 1569, in the reign of Elizabeth I, the Devon Muster Roll was compiled in order to provide a list of men and arms to defend the country against the threat of invasion by Spain. The presenters for Black Torrington were Thomas Parson, John Haysed, Lewis Burden and Christopher Elbury. Thomas Parson, of Beara, had married Agnes White in 1551. His son John, who was an attorney, married Winifred Davells in 1576. Thomas was taxed on income from land valued between £10 and £20. He had to provide one almain rivet (body armour), one harquebus (hand gun), one morion (helmet), one bow, one sheaf of arrows and one steel cap. John Haysed had to provide one almain rivet, two bows, two steel caps, one harquebus and one morion. Lewis Burden, Nicholas Stenlake, Robert and Richard Brawne, Thomas and Richard Olyver and John Kinge were all assessed on income from goods, valued at £10-20, to provide one bow, one sheaf of arrows, one bill and one steel cap each. The parish also had to provide 10 archers, 11 harquebusiers, 4 pikemen and 3 billmen. Richard Yorland, gentleman, was named among the archers.

In the same year as the Muster Roll Richard Bampfelde was instituted as Rector, in February 1569/70. He was presented by his namesake (another R. Bampfelde of Poltimore) after the death of Thomas Yonge. Mr Yonge was instituted in 1543 in the reign of Henry VIII and continued as Rector throughout the vicissitudes of the reigns of Edward VI and Mary Tudor and a constantly changing Prayer Book. Richard Bampfelde may never have come to Black Torrington, as he was also Rector of Poltimore from 1563-78. He probably had a curate, and a name is supplied in the parish registers, for among the marriages in 1580 is that of Thomas Slader, clerk in Holy Orders, who married Agnes the daughter of Lewis Burdon on 24th December. They had three children baptised at the parish church – Josyas, Benjamyn (who died in infancy) and Rebecca – between 1582-5.

Lewis Burdon lived at Long Hall. He made his will 24th December 1608 and died in January 1609/10. Although the will was not signed or sealed it was witnessed by Thomas Shutt, the Rector of Highampton, Stephen Burdon and William Parrish. Lewis Burdon described himself as an husbandman, implying that he was a tenant farmer. The farm was probably rented from the lord of the manor. Lewis, who was a scion of the Burdon family of Highampton, left to the poor of Highampton 5/- and to the poor of Black Torrington 10/-. He had five sons and three daughters baptized at Black Torrington between 1548 and 1574. He left to his eldest son, Leonard, one half of all his corn, to his grandson Lewis, "five silver spoons with images on the tops" (apostle spoons) and to his grandson John, "one heyfer yearling". He left to his second son, Robert, "1 cowe, 2 of my new silver spoons and 1 brass pan" and to his third son, John, "my little iron bound wheels, the other two new silver spoons and my red brass pan". He left to his youngest son, Steven, "three score pounds of money, 6 silver spoons and a brass pan bought of Richard Heale's children as well as the tenement called Longhall for the remainder of the original lease". He left to his daughter Agnes Slader £3.6s.8d., and to her daughter, Rebecca, £6.13.4., and "to all my grandchildren who are my godchildren, a sheep". To his wife Elizabeth he left "the best feather bed, 4 silver spoons, the new brazen pot and all money in her own keeping, and all plough stuff, dead stuff and household stuff for life". An inventory was made by his son-in-law, William Braunde, with John Payge, in February 1610, to the value of £215. It included "10 oxen, 2 steers, 10 kene, 2 heffers, 4 sterse, 6 yg cattle, 18 silver spoons, a musket and a callyver". (A caliver is a light musket). His widow, Elizabeth, died in 1617 and left her feather bed to her son John, and to Nell his wife (nee Smale) "my best wascott". She left the 4 silver spoons to her eldest son, Leonard, and to her daughter, Margaret Hitchin (or Hutching) she left "her best cott". Elizabeth signed the will with her mark.

William Braunde, who married Johane Burdon in 1572, died in 1616. A transcript of his will also survives. He left to his eldest son, Richard, 'my best bed and bedstead, my best table bord, my second best crocke, second best pan, my great iron bound wheels with $1/4$ of my plowstuffe, two platters, two pottagers (porringers), and one saucer, but my wife, Joan, to have all during her life if she remain unmarried'. To his son Leonard he left 'one bed, one crock, two platters, two pottingers, two saucers (all after the death or re-marriage of Joan) and £15. To his son Lewes he left 'my red brass pan, my best crocke, two platters, two pottingers and one saucer (again Joan was to have the continued use of them) and the £50 which I had lent him'. To his son William he left £5, and he left the sum of 3s.4d. each to his son John, his daughters Jane Smith and Elizabeth Hawden and to the poor of Black Torrington. The will was witnessed by John Oliver and Robert Burdon. His estate was valued at £244.17.8. It is not clear what relation this Braund was to the William Braund who was at **Keneland** (Kenneland) in the early part of the 16th century, and his grandson, Richard, who was living at Braundsworthy in the 1550s.

There was a tradition some years ago that the Braunds, who were very numerous in the Bucks Mills hamlet near Clovelly, were descended from survivors of the Spanish Armada in 1588 because of their dark and broad-headed features. These features are more probably derived from Mediterranean migrants of pre-Saxon times. The Braund Society (founded in 1982) believe they have a common ancestry in North Devon but so far have not found one earlier than William of Keneland in Black Torrington born circa 1465.

Taxation was again imposed, due to the increased threat of war, through the Subsidy Roll of 1581. Thomas Coham was taxed as a considerable landowner as well as Thomas Parson. William Braund and Henry Heessett appear as lesser landowners. Henry Hessett (or Heysed) was probably the brother of John Heysed who presented the 1569 Muster Roll. In 1567 Henry married

Catherine Haine and they had eight children baptized between 1568 and 1591. Henry died in 1593 and Katherine four months later. John Heysed had three children baptized between 1551 and 1562 (Johane, John and Philip). His son, John, died at Bridge in January 1597/8. It was unusual to indicate the place of death in the register, so it possibly meant that he did not die at home. Whether Bridge was a family property, or he was just visiting a neighbour, we do not know. Perhaps the Loveis family were already established at Bridge: they were certainly there later. John Heysett (it could have been either father or son) acted as attorney for John Davells of Marland in 1582 in the purchase of **Jenyns** (Jennings, an old property to the west of Fishleigh) for £60. Among those taxed on their goods in 1581 were Robert Braund (Robert Braund of Keneland, then in the parish of Black Torrington, died in 1588), John Heisett, Lewis Burdon, Richard Olyver, Christopher Elburie, John Kinge and John Smale. The Olivers lived at Graddon, and the Smales at Highweek.

In 1585 George Closse became Rector and stayed for thirty years until the reign of James I. The records do not state whom he succeeded so it is not known whether Mr Bampfelde remained as Rector until 1585 or not. Mr Closse was presented by Queen Elizabeth by virtue of a lapse in the patronage. He was a graduate of Trinity College, Cambridge. He had been a minister in London and was presented to the living of Cuckfield in Sussex in 1581, but was not instituted. In 1586 he was cited to preach a sermon at St Paul's Cross in London – whether he fulfilled his obligation is not known, for he appears to have resided in the parish. He had nine children baptized at Black Torrington between 1586 and 1603, and two of his daughters were married here: Sarah, to Henry Hazell in 1604, and Abigail to Robert Lopthorne in 1607. George Closse made a terrier of the church possessions in 1602 in which he states that Mr. Bampfielde of Poltimore was patron, and in which he estimates 164 acres of glebeland (of which some 55 acres remain today).

The Church in 1895.

It then included "a close to the north of the parsonage bounded on the east by the churchyard and on the west by Stephen Cohames land". South of the parsonage was little sanctuary and middle sanctuary (today called Centernhay) and south hill running down to Long Cross, "bounded on the east side by a lane or street to Holsworthy". Then Dukes close (on which are now built Long Cross cottages) and "on the east side of the lane to Okehampton and south of the lane leading to Smithsland, is Holy Well close of ten acres". Running up the hill to the south is "Higher Lyddalls and a little wood called Borrough bounded on the east by the lane to Okehampton. Beyond **Bearlands** (Beara), south of the highway to Hatherley, is a great close called Worthe moor of about 80 acres". Another terrier, dated 1612, is signed by Lewis Coham, churchwarden, and John Paige and James Limmbear, sidesmen. From 1591 George Closse was also Rector of Bradford. Mr. Closse was degraded in 1615 and deprived of both his livings. This was probably because of his increasing involvement with the local puritans who were quite numerous in North Devon at this time.

Black Torrington Mill c 1900

THE STUARTS AND THE CIVIL WAR

We may now conjecture what sort of place Black Torrington was at the end of the reign of Elizabeth I. We know that the church was here, not unlike it is at present, but thatched or slated. The Rectory stood where Bampfylde House is today. Not quite such a large house but still quite sizeable. It contained a parlour, hall, kitchen, dairy, two cellars, two butteries, seven chambers, one study, two clossetts, and one cockloft, with outhouses – a barn, stable, shippen and tool house – with walls of mud and stone and earthen flooring. Long Hall was a farmhouse, standing just below the churchyard. We know that The Poplars was an Elizabethan hall-house as it still has some of its original roof timbers. We can assume that Broad Street was already in existence (it is mentioned in 1628) with a lane running down to Kneela. To the east we would probably find Gorford (it was certainly there by 1660) and beside the river was the mill. Coham, of course, was standing and Beara and Bridge were gentlemen's residences. Buckpitt and Fishleigh and also Butterbear (which has now disappeared), Hayne, Forda and Highweek were farms. Round or near each farmstead would be a cluster of cottages for the farm labourers and servants. There were more distant farmsteads at Graddon, in Chilla (East Graddon Farmhouse still has late medieval roof timbers), Home Farm in West Chilla dates from the early 17th century, at Whiteley and at Braundsworthy. Altogether it was a parish of some four hundred people.

In 1615 Richard Bowden was presented to the living of Black Torrington by *Amisius Bampfelde* (Sir Amias Bampfylde of Poltimore was Sheriff of Devon in 1604) and was instituted on 5th August. He had been Rector of Poltimore from 1602-1606, and Rector of Huxham (next to Poltimore) from 1607-1615. Richard married firstly, Zenobia, daughter of Jonathan Prideaux of Thuborough in Sutcombe, and secondly Mary Bampfield of Poltimore, widow of Humphry Moore and younger daughter of Sir William Bampfield. The late Revd. John Powell (of Buckland Filleigh) believed that Richard was also the Richard Bowden who was Vicar of Okehampton from 1620 and held it in plurality with Black Torrington until his death in 1626. This may be borne out by the appearance of the name of another clergyman in the registers at this time.

In March 1619/20 John Byshopp, clerke, married Anne Yolland, and in July 1624 Mary, the daughter of John Bishopp, clerke, was baptized. John Bishoppe also signed the burial register in 1626. John Byshopp, a poor scholar who graduated at Exeter College in 1610 at the age of 22 years was Rector of Nymet Rowland (near Lapford) from 1619-21. He is also recorded as Vicar of Hittisleigh in 1642.

After the death of Richard Bowden the Bishop of Exeter presented Thomas Clifford to the living of Black Torrington, but he only held the office for one year. He was a Bachelor of Divinity of Exeter College, Oxford, and had been made a canon of Exeter Cathedral in 1625. In 1626 he was also appointed Vicar of Ilsington where he remained until his death in 1634. In addition he was the incumbent of Harberton from 1629-33, where he was succeded by his son, also Thomas, who died at the early age of 31 years in December 1637. His elder son, Hugh, was the father of another Thomas Clifford who was Lord High Treasurer to King Charles II and was created Baron Clifford of Chudleigh in 1673.

James Bampfylde, M.A., the next Rector, was the son of Sir Amyas (or Amisius) Bampfylde and was instituted into the family living in 1627 at the age of 26 years, after graduating at Oxford. In 1628 he made a terrier of the glebe lands of the Church of Black Torrington which he enjoyed "in peaceable possession – a house and garden between Broad Street and the land of Margarett Louvis, gentlewoman, on the north side and Thomas Coombe on the west". The terrier was signed by Abraham ffrye, churchwarden, and witnessed by John Smale. The glebe stretched south from the Rectory, including little 'centuary' and middle 'centuary' (George Closse wrote 'sanctuary'). In December 1634 James Bampfylde was instituted to the Vicarage of Rattery in south Devon. In September 1635 his daughter Dorothie was baptized at Black Torrington, and a second daughter, Elizabeth, was baptized here in February 1637/8. He had another daughter, Mary, and three sons, James, Edward and Benjamin. Between the years 1629-1632 he may have had a curate at Black Torrington for the name 'John Potter, clerke' appears in the registers.

There must be considerable doubt whether Mr. Bampfylde continued to live in Black Torrington after the 1630s. During this time the seeds of the Civil War were being sown. The attempt by Charles I to reign without Parliament for eleven years from 1629 meant that he had to devise new systems of taxation which were highly unpopular. The Scottish War in 1639 was an added burden. In 1641 the Parliamentarians drew up a 'Protestation' of dissatisfaction with the king and his Church, and the attempt to subvert the "Fundamental Laws of the land by Tyrannical Government". The Protestation concluded with a declaration to uphold the true reformed Protestant religion and to uphold "the Powers and Privileges of Parliament, the Lawful Rights of the Subjects". The form of Protestation was taken to every town and village in the spring of 1641. Among those signing in Black Torrington was 'John Courtier, minister'. John *Courteis* was named as a curate for James Bampfylde. Another minister is named in the burial register in 1643 when Mr. Stephen Webb, 'minister', was buried. We know the James Bampfylde was deprived of the living of Rattery in 1646 for contravening the ordinance against pluralities, and was later imprisoned in Dartmouth for some offence. He purchased his liberty for £50 and was restored to the living of Rattery at the Restoration in 1660. Throughout this time he held the living of Black Torrington, though he was obviously not resident throughout the period.

The Protestation form was signed in Black Torrington by 160 men, which would indicate a population for the parish of 400-450 – similar to that of today. In addition to parishioners it was also signed by John Westcombe, a glazier of Coleridge, who was "here at work". John Parsons, senior, did not sign being "sick in body and afflicted in mind abhors popery in practice and profession and therefore does desire further time to consider the protestation until God shall better able him being thereunto required". (The last Parsons recorded at Beara was John Parsons, gent, whose memorial of 1675 is now on the west wall of the church porch). Humphrey Smale signed as churchwarden, Stephen Coham and William Battin signed as Constables – a parochial office held in turn by principal householders of the parish – and William Cockram, Robert Hesed and George Smale signed as Overseers. Churchwardens, constables and overseers – who were charged with poor relief – were elected annually at the parish Vestry meeting. Stephen Coham, who was the grandson of the first Stephen, had married Susanna Smale, the daughter of Thomas Smale, in 1627. Humphrey Loveis, who signed, was designated a gentleman. Six other Smales signed including Robert of Leigh (Ley?). There were also eight Bickles including Robert Bickle Esq. and John Bickle of East Chilla, and seven Olivers, including John Oliver of East Chill [sic] and Robert Oliver of East Hill. Humphrey Kinge Esq. was one of four Kinges. Other familiar names on the list were Burdon (6), Paige (5), Frye (5), Braunde (4) and Risdon (3).

In the 1642 Assessment for tax James Bampfield, Rector, is rated at 70 shillings, Joan Parsons at 41s. and John Parsons, gent., at 21s. Probably John Parsons, senior, had died since the Protestation of the previous year. John Harris of Stowford, who was lord of the Manor, was assessed at 25s. as was Thomas Oliver: Stephen Coham and William Cockram were assessed at 22s., Humphrey Loveis at 21s. and Lewis Burdon at 20s.6d. Thomas Mallet, sergeant at law, was assessed at 18s. and Nicholas Mallet Esq. at 9s. The Mallets of Somerset owned property in Black Torrington; their ancestor, John Mallet of Beaford, married Zenobia Davells in the 16th century.

The Civil War, which began in August 1642, does not seem to have impinged to any noticeable extent on the history of Black Torrington. In April 1643 there was an encounter between Royalist forces, led by Sir Ralph Hopton, advancing into Devon from Cornwall and a small detachment of

Parliamentary soldiers under the command of James Chudleigh. 4000 foot soldiers and 500 horse, many of them raw recruits, were approaching Sourton Down when the vanguard was attacked by 108 men who were scattered on the Down in six small groups. Many of the inexperienced recruits threw down their arms and fled and the main royalist force retreated to Bridestowe leaving 60 dead on the field. In May, in the same year, Sir Bevil Grenville led his troops to victory against the Parliamentarian army, which was under the command of Lord Stamford, at Stratton by Bude. There was another skirmish, closer at hand when Sir Francis Doddington routed a troop of Parliament soldiers on Hatherleigh moor in September 1644. By February 1645/6 Ralph Hopton (now Baron Hopton) had been made commander-in-chief and was surprised at Great Torrington by Sir Thomas Fairfax leading the New Model Army and was defeated. On 23rd February the New Model Army passed through Holsworthy on its way from Torrington to Cornwall. And that is as near as the fighting seems to have reached.

Among the gentry of the parish at this time was the Loveis family. Humfrey Loveis was certainly living at Bridge in the 17th century. The first mention of the family in Black Torrington is in the 16th century when Mr. Leonard *Lovys* had four children baptized here between 1555-1560. This may be the same Leonard Loveys who built Ogbeare Hall in the parish of North Tamerton during the reign of Queen Elizabeth I, and died in 1575/6 leaving at least four sons: Thomas, William, Humfrey and Richard who are mentioned in his will. He was a brother of John Loveys who was a citizen and mercer of London. Leonard was the owner of several manors in Devon and Cornwall, including that of High Hampton. The name Loveis appears again in the Black Torrington records at the beginning of the 17th century when four children of Humfry Loveys were baptized between 1605–1612. Margarett *Louvis* is mentioned in the Rector's terrier of 1628 as a land-owner. The manor of High *Heanton* (High Hampton) was sold by Humfrey Loveis of Black Torrington in 1630. This Humprey died in 1650 when he was living at Bridge. His son, Humfrey, who married Philippa Morcombe of Sheepwash in 1629, predeceased his father, dying in 1635. At this time another John *Loves*, gentleman, had five children baptized at Black Torrington between 1633–1639. One of these, Samuel, was buried here in 1713, and is the last entry of that name in the church records.

THE RESTORATION AND INTO THE 18th CENTURY

After the Civil War the Commonwealth was established in 1649 and the Prayer Book was forbidden. What happened in Black Torrington? The record is silent. James Bampfylde continued to be Rector throughout the Civil War; he returned to Black Torrington sometime before his death. Baptisms, marriages and burials continued, but we do not know whether the new Directory of Worship was used in place of the Prayer Book. Mr. Bampfylde died and was buried in Black Torrington in May 1663, three years after the restoration of the monarchy. His will is dated 21st May, and he was buried on 23rd. He left £80 to his daughter, Dorothy, and his library to his daughter Mary. He left £50 each to his sons Edward and Benjamin and the residue to his son James, with his widow, Wilmot, to have his household goods for life. He was succeeded by James Lake, B.A., who was instituted in October 1663 and on the same day was married at Black Torrington to Elizabeth Bampfyld, the middle daughter of James. James and Elizabeth Lake had two sons, Bampfyld, baptized in February 1664/5 and James, baptized in March 1673/4. Elizabeth died in October of the same year. There is a memorial slate, broken but still legible, to the memory of Elizabeth and James Lake, which is now fixed to the east exterior wall of the church. (Before the church restoration in 1900 this tablet was set in the floor of the chancel). Higher up on the same wall is a lead plaque inscribed "James Lake, *Recttor*, 1708". This presumably commemorates some restoration of the church, possible rebuilding of the chancel, at that date.

James Lake's father was also named James. He was a canon of Exeter and Rector of Aveton Gifford, in south Devon, when he died in 1678. He was possessed of a house in St. Sidwells Street, Exeter, and James, junior, had a parcel of 106 books belonging to his father in his custody. Father and son were both graduates of Oxford and the third James also matriculated, at Jesus College in March 1691/2, but does not seem to have graduated. He did however marry and two sons were baptized in Black Torrington in 1709 and 1712.

In which year Mr. James Lake, Rector, died and was buried here on 9th January 1712/3. Benoni Bampfylde, whose fine slate memorial is placed on the south wall of the sanctuary of the church, died in July 1721. He was possibly the grandson of James Bampfylde. His will was dated 29th June, 1721. He left £10 to James Lake, son of the late Rector, and £20 each to James' sons (James and John). Their father and Stephen Coham were to be the boys' trustees until their 21st birthdays.

The Stephen Coham, who signed the Protestation form in 1641, died in 1655, leaving by his will to his wife Susanna, £20 a year for life: "to my daughter Margaret *Heised* 6d, to my daughters Ruth, Mary, Julian and Susanna each £140 at the age of 24 years". The residue was left to his only son (and heir) Lewis. Susanna died, without inheriting, at the age of 23 years. Margaret had married John Heassett in 1651 and Julian (or Jyllian) married his brother, Joakim Hessett in 1665. Lewis married Mary, the daughter of John Arscott of Tetcott, in 1669. Their two elder sons, Stephen and John, married the two daughters and co-heiresses of William Holland of Upcott Avenel in Sheepwash. Robert de Holand had married one of the daughters of Alan la Zouch at the beginning of the 14th century. William Holland's grandfather had married the heiress of Thorne in Holsworthy and therefore the Coham estates were considerably increased. Stephen Coham married Mary Holland in 1706, and John Coham married Margaret Holland in 1712. It was about this time that Coham was destroyed by fire and the family moved their seat to Upcott Avenel, not returning to Coham until about the year 1779. John and Margaret Coham settled at Bovacott in Bradford. Both Stephen and John were to be fathers of clergymen. Holland, the youngest son of Stephen, born in 1720, married Christina, the daughter of James Silke, Rector of Buckland Filleigh: Holland Coham was Rector of Northlew from 1750–1777. Arthur, the fourth son of John Coham, became Archdeacon of Wiltshire, and Rector of Brixton Deverill from 1781 until he died in 1799. Arthur, the younger brother of Stephen and John, married Elizabeth Burdon of Highampton in 1715. Mary, the elder sister of the brothers, married Benoni Bampfylde of Ley (a small hamlet between Coham and Lana) in 1704. He died in 1721 as mentioned above.

James Lake died in 1712. His successor was John Bradford who was instituted on 20th January 1712/3, eleven days after the burial of Mr. Lake! He was presented by Sir Coplestone Warwick Bampfylde, Bart. He married Blanch, the daughter of John Glubb of Great Torrington. A son, Peter, was buried in February 1722/3, and a daughter, Blanch, baptized in November 1723. There were two other children baptized: Richard in 1727 and Elizabeth in 1731. The Revd. Mr. John Bradford, Rector, was buried 9th March 1736/7. On 24th May 1737 John Carew, M.A. was instituted to the living, presented by Sir Richard Warwick Bampfylde, Bart. (Sir Coplestone died in 1727). John Carew may have been a cousin of the patron: Sir Coplestone's wife was Gertrude Carew.

*Higher Braundsworthy at the turn of the century.
Probably Mr & Mrs Henry Ham.*

Beara Court after rebuilding by Mr. L. Reichel.

Coham House, West Front after rebuilding c. 1870

He was ordained priest in December 1733, and in 1744 he answered the Archdeacon's Visitation questions for Black Torrington. He stated that he resided in the parsonage and that there were no dissenters in the parish and no school. There were two services in the church on Sundays, with a sermon in the morning. The sacrament was given at Easter, Whitsun, Michaelmas and Christmas, at which there were about 30 communicants. The catechism was taught in Lent. He either died or resigned the living in 1762.

Some years before the Restoration there was established in Black Torrington a benefaction for the beautifying and repair of the parish church. The earliest mention of it is in a deed dated February 1662/3 when John *Brand* and two others (not named) granted their trusteeship, or enfeoffment, to Samuel Loveis and others. The property of the trust consisted of six closes (or meadows) and nine houses which were "the enfeoffment and gift of John Coham, deceased, to hold. . . . for the use and benefit of the church of Black Torrington". It is not certain which John Coham made this gift. The John who was the direct ancestor of the present family died in 1557. Most of the houses were in Broad Street; one was "a house above the well", this may be identified as the well that was opposite the Public Hall. In the 18th century and in the early part of the 19th century two of these properties were let to the Overseers of the Poor as Parish Poor houses. The fields were respectively off Back Lane and below Kneela and the present gardens of Rose Cottage and The Briary. By the 19th century there were twelve dwellings in the possession of the trustees of the Church Lands, but all the property was sold during the next 100 years apart from four fields and a garden. Proceeds of sales in the 20th century were invested and by the end of the century brought an income to the charity of over £1500 a year. The income from rents in 1885 was £44.

In 1722 the surviving feoffees, John Burdon of Highampton, gent., Stephen Coham of *Shipwash*, gent. and George Paige of Black Torrington, yeoman, nominated Charles Burdon, an attorney of Black Torrington and younger brother of Robert Burdon of Burdon in Highampton, as their successor. There is a bound volume of accounts of the feoffees and churchwardens of Black Torrington from 1736-1883. In 1736 Christopher Durrant paid £2.2s. a year to rent Reedyparke (1.5 acres). House rents ranged from 5s. to 1s.4d. (25p to 7p) a year. The big expense of that year was £4.2s.6d. paid to John Hatherly for providing and laying 1,100 shingles (roof-tiles), and £2.10s. for the clerk's annual wages. Another annual payment for some years was £1.6s.8d. for bread and wine for the year's sacrament. The sexton (at first called the doorkeeper) was paid 6s. a year and the glazier 10s. Others who worked on the church were Barnabas May, the carpenter, and John Burdon, the mason. John Hatherly was sometimes assisted by his brother Philip and by John Allin. The carpenters were paid 1s. 4d. a day, and Richard Parsons and Hugh Balkwill were paid 1s. a day for work in the churchyard and mending hedges. Richard Parsons was the sexton, and an earlier Hugh Balkwill (uncle?), who died in

1725, was the parish clerk. All these tradesmen who worked about the church were resident in the parish, and their names appear in the register of baptisms and burials. In 1738 new seats were made for the singers at a cost of £5.12s.6d. Other regular expenses included washing and repairing the surplice, new bell ropes, repairing the windows and attention to the bells, oil and candles. In 1740 a new Common Prayer book was purchased for 15s. The purchase was repeated in 1751 and 1761. A regular expense was incurred every 5th November when 10s. was paid for the ringers and supplying them ale. In 1746 a similar sum was paid for ringing for the Duke's victory over the rebels (the battle of Culloden). Occasional payments of one shilling (sometimes more) were made to vagrants in distress: sailors, or men and women who had suffered loss from fire or flood. In 1743 £10 was spent on restoration work on the tower. In 1746 James Allen was paid £1.17s. 6d. for the new Church Gate. In 1751 Humphrey Perkin was paid £11.10s. for casting 92 feet of lead: on this occasion Thomas Marsh was the carpenter, John Balsdon the mason and Henry Bond the smith. Again all of them were parishioners, and Thomas, the son of Henry Bond, was to rent a 'Churchlands house' at a later date. As well as these tradesmen there were two shoemakers in the village in the mid-18th century: Joseph Chapman, who married Joan Stenlake in 1751 (and who was the progenitor of the Chapman family of Black Torrington), and John Millford. In 1753 Mr Lewis Coham paid 6s.8d. for 'breaking of the ground in the Church' for the burial of William Coham, gent., of Bideford. It appears that the families of the gentry and leading yeomen were often buried within the church, not in a vault, but just under the floor. Also in 1753 the sum of 1s.6d. was spent on the Bradford singers – what event brought them to Black Torrington is not stated – but over the ensuing years there were repeated payments to singers, from Thornbury, Sheepwash, and Halwill, as well as Bradford.

It is not clear whether Rector John Carew resigned in 1762 and died shortly afterwards, or whether he died in office. John Burgess was instituted in August 1762 (he had been ordained priest in December 1750). He was the son of William Burgess, gentleman, of North Molton. He entered Exeter College, Oxford, in May 1743 and was awarded his B.A. in 1746. He did not immediately come to live in Black Torrington but continued to live in Filleigh in North Devon, at Castle Hill, and served as curate at West Buckland. He wrote in the Visitation return of 1764 that the previous incumbent died in poor circumstances and the Parsonage needed to be rebuilt, and he 'had not yet received money enough to repair it'. In the interim the parish was being served by the Rector of North Lew, Mr. Holland Coham, at a stipend of £20 per annum, ' and had been served by neighbouring clergy for several years'. Mr. Burgess intended to move to Black Torrington immediately after Easter, where there was 'a service every Sunday and two in the summer, with sermon in the morning'. The church was in good repair, but 'I can find no terrier, but will make one'. There were 110 families in the parish, but no chapel nor papists; no school, no almshouses or library. There was 'land given for the Church which produced a rent of £5.13s.6d., and some land for the poor with a rent providing £2.7s.10p. (this was Speccot's Charity). There were about 40 communicants four times a year, and he expected to have 30 persons for confirmation. In 1764, 56 persons from Black Torrington were confirmed at Bideford by Bishop Keppel. Fifteen years later, in 1779, John Burgess completed another return stating that 'he took one service each Sunday at Black Torrington and one service at Halwill', for which he was paid £20 p.a. The catechism was held in the summer, and there were 40-50 communicants. There was a terrier! Had he made one or found one of the old ones? He died in September 1780, at the age of 56. His memorial tablet is in the chancel of the church and it records his "exemplary piety. . . equally respected by rich and poor. . . a generous benefactor. . . a character worthy of imitation".

During Mr Burgess' incumbency, in the year 1770, Samuel and Jonas *Honkin* were paid £8 'for Plaistering the Church'. Samuel Hunkin was the son of Jonas and Sarah Hunkin of Shebbear; he was baptized at Black Torrington in 1724. Many of his descendants were masons or stonecutters, and at least two emigrated to America. Others farmed here or in neighbouring parishes throughout the 19th and 20th centuries: at Buckpitt, Week Park, Graddon, Rightadown, Down, Westover and, most recently, Ralph Hunkin at Long Cross. One of Samuel's sons (another Samuel) farmed at Buckpitt; his daughter Susannah married Thomas Harris. Two of their sons, having completed their apprenticeship as wheelwrights with John Jury, left the village in the early 1870s on foot to look for work. They walked as far as Newcastle-upon-Tyne! Here they started a coach building business which flourished. Samuel Harris returned to Devon after the death of his first wife and married, in 1896, his childhood sweetheart, Susan Isaac who had been born at Kneela in 1856, and was the sister of William Spear Isaac.

In 1772 four of the six bells in the tower were taken down to be re-cast, with added metal, by John Pennington at a cost of £74.7s.10p. to which was added the cost of a new frame for the bells and floor for the bell chamber, new ropes, carriage and ale for the workers amounting to £20.4s.8d. The Penningtons were originally a Cornish family of bell founders. The first was Bernard Pennington who was mayor of Bodmin in 1666. In the next century there were Penningtons at Lezant and later at Stoke Climsland, and they cast nearly 500 bells between 1710-1818. The Devon branch of the family, led by Thomas and John Pennington, cast nearly as many in a similar period. Although based in Exeter the casting was often done near the church, wherever there was deep clay and sufficient bell-metal was provided by the parish. The 1772 bells were founded at Northlew: George Hatherleigh was paid for two days work to help drawing the bells to Northlew and bringing them home. We do not know the age of the bells that were recast. In 1553 Black Torrington had only three bells in the tower; at a later date the peal was made up to six. In 1856 the tenor and fourth bells were recast (the tenor was reported as being cracked in 1852). This time the work was done by C. & G. Mears of London. The railway had come to Devon (the Barnstaple line was opened in 1854) and the bells were carried to Copplestone. Mr Mears' bill for the two bells was £36.0s.8d. The total cost, including railway carriage and the re-hanging, was £65. This was met by a public subscription, which raised £35.17s., and a 3d. rate. The subscription list was headed by Llewellyn Llewellyn Esq. of Buckland House, the then Lord of the Manor, who gave £10. Bickford Coham Esq. and Mr Veale, the curate, gave £2 each. Holland Coham Esq. and George Coham Esq., George Risdon and John Tanton, the Churchwardens, Mr. Owen, the doctor, Messrs Tucker, Horrell, Sparke and Paige and Mr Heysett of Bovacott each gave £1. In all there were 80 subscribers, the others giving sums ranging from 10s.6d. to 1s.

On Mr Burgess' death in 1780 there followed a brief incumbency by the Revd. Denys Yonge who stayed only two years. He was also Rector of Morwenstow and had permission to live at Great Torrington. The only event of note during Mr Yonge's time was the purchase of 'a new flagon, bason and plate for the sacrament'. Mr Abraham was paid £1.6s.8d. for supplying them in 1782. The pewter flagon is still in the possession of the Church and is inscribed with the name of the churchwarden, John Stenlake. It was not until 1790 that the parish seems to have appointed two churchwardens. There is a complete list of churchwardens from the year 1736 (see appendix 5). Until 1790 most of them served for two years; occasionally one and sometimes three. John Stenlake was an exception, serving five years (1781-86). He had married Elizabeth, the daughter of Richard Oliver of Addlehole in Chilla, in 1754. Addlehole was part of East Lake in East Chilla. Richard Oliver was churchwarden in 1738. Richard Stenlake, son of John and Elizabeth, still owned East Lake in 1843, but no longer lived in Chilla.

On 16th June 1783 the Revd. Richard Warwick Bampfylde was instituted to the living of Black Torrington, being presented by his brother, Sir Charles Warwick Bampfylde. He had been ordained priest only the day before. Mr Bampfylde was just 24 years old, and in November that year was also instituted to the livings of Huxham and Poltimore, where he resided. The name Courtenay Pierce appears in the church registers from 1785-1789, and he was presumably Mr Bampfylde's curate. William Holland Coham signs in 1790 and is named as curate in the 1798 visitation return, being licensed with a stipend of £40 per annum. At this date services were held twice on Sundays, with the sacrament four times a year with about 30 communicants. There were then 100 families in the parish, no dissenting chapel, but there was a private school. William Holland Coham, who became Rector of Halwill in 1807, continued as curate of Black Torrington and resided at Coham.

THE 19th CENTURY

The nineteenth century saw great changes in the population figures. In the census of 1801 the number was 706; by 1841 the population reached its maximum at 1252. The last quarter of the century witnessed a sharp fall with the decline of agriculture, and in 1901 the number was 652 (these figures include the Eastern and Western hamlets of Totleigh and Middlecot which were transferred to Highampton and Bradford respectively for civil purposes in 1884). At the turn of the century it is possible to identify some of the tradesmen living and working in the parish. James Paige was the miller at Black Torrington and Thomas Rockey was the miller at Totleigh. There were three blacksmiths in the village – Shadrach Spry, William Clemetts and John Dart – and James Luxton at Cripple. There were three shoemakers – Abraham Harris, William Heysett and Francis Johns. John Sillifant and John Squire were stonemasons. Joseph Johns, William and John Allin, Henry and Thomas Marsh were carpenters and William Brent was a joiner. Joseph Bailey and Nicholas Jeffery were tailors and James Dawe a butcher. Faithful Lane, whose son James moved to Bradford, was the clock and watch-maker. Richard Heard was a painter and Abraham Hockin was a cooper. George Wonnacott was a plumber and glazier. He does not appear to have lived in the parish, but was regularly paid for jobs about the church.

The 1841 census names one of three cottages near Black Torrington bridge, where Kingsley Cottage now stands, 'tanyard' but as to when it was used and who the tanner was there is no record.

Later in the 19th century George Braund was at Black Torrington Mill and then Henry Down. As well as Shadrack Spry and John Dart there were four other blacksmiths in the village – Arthur Petherick, James Saunders, James Paige and John Hearn. Another John Dart was a smith at King's Moor as also was James Down at Chilla. Samuel Vanstone, and later, Isaac Lewis, George Denford (from Hatherleigh) and Samuel May (from Sheepwash) were shoemakers, while Benjamin Wooldridge carried on the trade in Chilla. John Ward, Edmund and Samuel Hunkin were masons and Emmanuel Horn a builder. Among the carpenters and wheelwrights were Samuel Jury, and later

Squire George Coham 1802–1878

his son John, James Vanstone, Robert Down and Philip Andrew, and at Chilla James Down's brother John. William Isaac was the butcher and Thomas Braund was a plumber. John Johns was a thatcher and John Kelly and William Letheren at Long Hall were the saddlers. There were two drapers and grocers – William Chapman and William Hall, while John Gay kept a shop at Chilla. There was a baker, Mary Gilbert, and a dressmaker, Charity Vanstone, and an auctioneer, James Gilbert. This was a new profession to be found in a country village in the mid-19th century. There were also two milliners – Mary Gilbert's daughter (also Mary) and Grace Marsh. The farrier (and veterinary surgeon) was John Sanders at Windmilland, whose father, from Highampton, had been a farrier before him. At this time, and until the end of the century, many women were employed as out-workers for the glove makers of Torrington. In 1850 there were nine glove-making businesses in Great Torrington. Harrods Directory for 1878 states that Arthur Southcombe had a glove factory in Sheepwash. Two nurses are recorded towards the end of the century. Mrs Susanna Paige was lodging with constable Milverton at the police house in 1881, and Susan Balsdon was a 'sick nurse', living near the chapel in 1891.

Among the yeomen farmers at the beginning of the century were James Tanton at Hayne, George Paige at Bridge, James Risdon at Butterbear (the son of John Risdon, formerly of Buckland Filleigh, who had leased it from the lord of the manor in 1759), Samuel Hunkin at Buckpitt, Elias Leach at Highweek, Richard Balsdon at Trew, John Stenlake at Hoop and East Chilla, John Yelland at West Chilla, Amos Parsons at Graddon and Joseph Chapman (son of the earlier Joseph) who is titled 'yeoman' in the Feoffees Book in 1799, though it is not clear what land he held at this time. All these men, with the exception of Risdon, Hunkin and Yelland, were, at one time or another, churchwardens. Another Risdon from Buckland Filleigh bought Hayne and Blackley in the 1820s. This was George Smale Risdon, who in April 1827, advertised in the *Exeter Flying Post* a sale at the Union Inn of 636 oak trees, 5 elm and 2 ash, of large dimensions suitable for a ship builder or timber merchants.

With the tithe map of 1843 it is possible to identify the landowners as well as the tenants. The principal landowner was Lord Ashburton, the lord of the manor, who had over 1,000 acres of farm land. The largest of the manor farms, nearly 300 acres, was High Week, where the tenant was Richard Leach. John Hopper farmed 235 acres at Lana and Elias Leach had 190 acres at Forda. Joseph Risdon had succeeded to Butterbeare (150 acres) and George Risdon, who owned 160 acres at Hayne and Blackley, rented another 160 acres at Hillmoor. Arscott Braund was the tenant of 120 acres at Fraunch as well as holding 130 acres at Braundsworthy from his father (W. Hockin Braund). The Coham family were the next largest landowners in the parish, although they now lived at Dunsland which was inherited, by the marriage of William Holland Coham to Mary Bickford in 1790, at the death of Arscott Bickford in 1817. The main farms of the Coham estate in Black Torrington were West

John Daw 1760–1849

Chilla (200 acres) farmed by John Walter, and Buckpitt, where Samuel Hunkin farmed 85 acres. Coham House and the home farm (120 acres) were leased to John G. Maxwell, but the farm was taken over by Richard Born in 1850. In the Western Hamlet there were 150 acres at Middlecot farmed by George and Stephen Ward. John Woollcombe of Ashbury was another landowner; he had Whiteleigh (250 acres) and Lower Whiteleigh (140 acres) farmed by John Hutchings and James Gilbert.

The largest owner-occupier was George Paige with 225 acres at Bridge, followed by the Rector who had 190 acres of glebe, with John Horrell owning 130 acres at East Chilla. Lewis Heysett of Bovacott owned East Graddon (120 acres let to George Piper). In the Eastern Hamlet James Tanton owned 213 acres at East Totleigh and Anthony Tucker has 184 acres at Totleigh Barton. John Burdon of Burdon owned 90 acres at West Chilla (let to John Knight), and Hole Farm, a similar acreage, farmed by William Horn. The two other sizeable farms in the parish were East Lake where Benjamin Wooldridge farmed 170 acres owned by Richard Stanlake, and Beara (155 acres) farmed by James Johns, rented from Lewis Buck of Bideford, who was M.P. for North Devon 1839-57. His father was a grandson of Sara Stucley and married Ann Orchard of Hartland Abbey. His son, George Stucley Buck inherited both Hartland and the Affeton estates of the Stucleys. He was created a baronet in 1859 and took the name Stucley.

Recorded among the gentry was the Revd. William Holland Coham at Coham (whose memorial tablet is on the north wall of the nave of the church). He was the youngest son of the Revd. Holland Coham, and was Rector of Halwill as well as acting as assistant curate for the absent Rector, Richard Bampfylde. He was also very interested in agriculture. Charles Vancouver, who published *General View of Agriculture in Devon* in 1808, visited Coham and Dunsland and described Mr Coham as "this spirited improver and truly valuable man". He went on to say that Mr Coham wrote that "the condition of the working class in his district was as wretched as anywhere in the kingdom". Wages were low and the decline of wool-spinning, owing to the use of spinning machinery, had almost halved the income of labourers. John Denis Burdon, son of the Black Torrington attorney Charles Burdon, appears to have lived at Upcott before he built the house now known as The Larches in about 1812. He had inherited Burdon House in Highampton when his father died in in 1787, but it seems that he never lived there. He later inherited property in Kenton near Exeter where he died in 1842. He was buried at Black Torrington where his memorial may be seen in the church. One of the employees of Charles Burdon in 1776 was John Daw his clerk. In 1789 John Daw left for East Budleigh to work for the Rolle family, becoming steward to Lord Rolle in 1796. He was enrolled at Gray's Inn in 1806 and himself became a lawyer. On his death in 1849 he bequeathed a pair of cottages in Broad Street to the Rector and Churchwardens, which are the origin of Daw's Charity. In 1823 he erect-

Kingsley Cottage

ed a table top memorial over the grave of his parents, John and Patience who died in the 1790s, which lies just to the left of the church entrance. Also included among the gentry were Lewis Braund at Braundsworthy and James Hearn who came from Shebbear and married Anne Risdon of Buckland Filleigh; they lived for a while in Black Torrington before returning to Shell House in Shebbear. In 1786 and 1787 he was paid £1.13s. for instructing the singing in the parish church, and again in 1789 when he was paid £1.16s.6d. for 'showing the singers'. He was churchwarden, with George Braund, in 1803. A memorial to James Hearn and his wife Anne is placed on the wall of the south aisle in the parish church, where there is also a memorial to George Braund.

By the middle of the nineteenth century William Holland Bickford Coham was living at Dunsland in Bradford (the Revd. William Bickford Coham had died in 1847). His uncle George was living at Upcott Avenel in Sheepwash. John Burdon had moved to Kenton, and his new house (not named The Larches until the 1870s) was occupied by the Misses Peacock from Northamptonshire. Their finely carved Delabole slate memorials lie, enclosed by rusting railings, to the west of the church tower. William Hockin Braund was at Braundsworthy where he died in 1863. Mr Joseph Chapman who was a timber merchant and owned some property in the parish had moved to Sheepwash. The Revd. Westcott Veale was living at the Rectory.

Milking time in the farmyard: George Dennis and family at Hole Farm in the early 1900s

The Back Drive to Coham

THE LORDS OF THE MANOR

The last mention of the lordship of the manor was when it passed from the Davils to Harris of Hayne in Stowford at the end of the 16th century. It remained in that family until the eighteenth century and was then exchanged with a cousin, Harris of Castle Park in Lifton. In the 1832 William Arundell Harris Arundell (having taken the surname of the Arundells of Kynegie in Cornwall) of Lifton sold the manor of Black Torrington to discharge a mortgage. In 1843 it was in the possession of Alexander Baring, Lord Ashburton, who died in 1848 and it then passed to his son. Lord Ashburton had also bought the manor of Buckland Filleigh, and its estates, from the Fortescue family with the residence at Buckland House (in 1832), although his main residence was in Hampshire.

In 1854 the manors of Black Torrington and Buckland Filleigh were purchased by Llewellyn Llewellyn Esq, who resided at Buckland House. His widow sold the manors and estates in 1861 to Thomas Fisher Esq. who lived at Buckland House until the late 1870s. In 1881 the Lordship of the manor of Black Torrington had changed again having been purchased by David Clarke Esq. of Macclesfield, whose agent and steward was Mr Joseph Chapman. One of the daughters of Joseph Chapman had a record of a meeting of the Court Leat and Court Baron of David Clarke in June 1889. The Portreeve was Mr Chapman and the Steward was Mr Groves Cooper. Mr George Risdon was the foreman of the jury that consisted of Messrs Edwin Risdon, James Sparke, John Kelly, Emanuel Horn, Samuel Hutchings, William Yelland, Isaac Vanstone, Richard Balsdon, William Letheren, John Isaac and Lewis Isaac. After the officers had surveyed the bounds of the manor and found everything satisfactory they retired to the Commercial Hotel for dinner. Mr Risdon, who was then 93 years of age and died in the following August, spoke of the many improvements to the village since the manor was in the possession of Mr Clarke. Miss Chapman related that the Court Leat due to be held in 1901 was prevented by the flooding of the Torridge, and the steward and his companions, unable to cross, were entertained by Mr Hobbs at Gortleigh. The Revd. John Powell recorded the overflow of the Torridge in November 1894 when 'several cottages and Black Torrington flour-mills were flooded, and Mr Corney of Halwill was swept away trying to cross Black Torrington bridge; he was carried 3/4 mile towards Sheepwash and not rescued until the next morning'!

David Clarke died, intestate, in 1894. His heirs were three daughters and a grandson and the manor estate was put up for sale. It included the farms of Butterbear, Highweek, Forda and Lana, West Chilla and Northcote, with Long Hall, Torridge House and 24 cottages. Highweek and Northcote were bought by their respective tenants, Richard Baily and George Blight. Forda and Lana and nine cottages were unsold and were put up again in 1902. Mr John Fleming bought the lordship of the manor and made a present of it to his daughter-in-law, Elinor Coham-Fleming, the grand daughter of the Revd. W.B. Coham and the only child of Mr W.H. Bickford Coham, who had re-built Coham in the 1870s with a new West front.

The record of the Courts Leat held by Col. John Blyth Coham-Fleming from 1903-1918 have been preserved. The steward throughout this time was Mr Apsley Petre Peter and the court was held at the Union Inn in May. In 1903 the jurymen were Joseph Chapman, foreman, Samuel Broad, A.J. Isaac, John Jury, snr., John Jury, jnr., George Martin, James Risdon, William Hunkin, John Kelly, A.J.Kelly and Edred Kelly. They perambulated the bounds noting the

Long Hall c. 1890. John Kelly, saddler, on pony; possibly his wife and daughters on right

pump in The Larches wall, for which an acknowledgement of 6d. should be paid by the Sanitary Committee; the poor state of the fencing around some of the Lord's wastes; that Richard Parsons was stacking wood on the waste at Long Cross without paying rent; that sawdust from Jury's saw-pit was blocking the water-table; that the pump opposite the shop should be brought nearer the road and a clear way should be left for the glebe footpath. The last Court was held at the Union Inn on 23rd May 1918. Those named as jurors were G. Copplestone, foreman, Herbert Chapman, Ernest Chapman, John Jury, A.J.Isaac, E.W.Kelly, A.J.Kelly, N.Heard (Golden Inn), B. Hopper (Wonford), William Hooper, Joseph Chapman and B.Hutchings (Hole Moor).

Mr & Mrs William Coham-Fleming at Coham, 1992

Union Hotel in the time of William Hockin circa 1880

Woodhills Brewery (on the site of the Public Hall) c. 1890

THE VILLAGE INNS

The earliest name recorded for a landlord of the Union Inn (now the Torridge Inn) is Philip Gilbert, who was named as the licensee from 1822-25. He was also the Parish clerk, which position he seems to have held from 1806 until his death in 1828. Philip Gilbert married Mary Buckpitt in 1795 and their son, James, lived at Gilbert's Terrace, where now stands Briary Cottage opposite the Parish Hall. James Gilbert practised as an auctioneer in Black Torrington until his death in 1855. Although 1822 is the earliest record of the Union Inn by name it was certainly there a long time before that date. The name possibly commemorates the union of England and Scotland in 1707. It has been suggested that the name comes from the 'Holsworthy Union', of which Black Torrington was a sub-district, but the union of parishes to administer the Poor Law did not occur before 1836 (though it could refer to the union of Great Britain and Ireland in 1801). Philip Gilbert, whose name appears on the 1822 licence, is described as a victualler in the Baptism Register of the parish church in May 1814 when his younger son Richard was baptized.

In the 1730s four people held licences in Black Torrington: Ann Balkwell, Richard Furse, Elizabeth Risdon and John Squire. Unfortunately the licences do not identify the premises, but from the Tithe Apportionment map of 1843 we can identify three: the Union Inn (now the Torridge), the Pack Horse, two doors further along the street (now a house called Claremont) and a beer house at King's Moor Cross on the Holsworthy Road. At this date James Osborn rented the Union Inn from the Coham estate, having held the licence from 1826. He continued there until he died in 1851, when his widow, Elizabeth, took the licence and continued there for at least ten years. In 1870 Elizabeth Ashton was the licensee but in 1872 the licence was granted to William Hockin of Plymouth. William was born in Black Torrington where his father, Abraham, was a cooper (barrel maker). When William died in 1887 the licence passed to his son Henry. In 1888 Henry established a skittle ground in the plot beside the inn which gave rise to complaints. The Churchlands trustees, whose land it was, required that there should be no play after 10 p.m. In 1903 Henry is reported as having left the country owing £1 to the Churchlands trustees for rent.

In 1830 a song was written by John Madge of Highampton for the Devon county election of that year, following the death of George IV. It was printed in Hatherleigh and features the part the Union Inn played in the electioneering by the Revd. William Bickford Coham and his brother George Coham of Upcott Avenel on behalf of the Whig, Lord Ebrington (the son of Earl Fortescue) and Sir Thomas Acland against the Tory, Mr Edmund Bastard of Kitley. Only a third of the whole is printed here:

Parson Coham and his brother George,
Two worthy gentlemen,
They both did play an active part,
Their country to defend, my boys,
Their country to defend, my boys.

Their valour did display
For Sir Thomas and Lord Ebrington,
That they might gain the day, my boys,
That they might gain the day.

Parson Coham did get many votes,
It was hundreds I am sure,
And on the tenth of August
He met them on Hill Moor.
Their hats were decked with laurel,
His coach was trimmed so gay:
He marched them into Black Torrington,
And the band did sweetly play,
And the band did sweetly play.

When they came into Black Torrington
Such a sight was never seen,
To see those Votes take breakfast,
All at the Union Inn,
Parson Coham was so delighted,
He to the votes did say,
"Sir Thomas and Lord Ebrington
I hope will gain the day,
I hope will gain the day, my boys."

When the breakfast it was over
Parson Coham he was so kind
To give those votes a bumper
Of the best of Osbourne's wine;
He says, my men come drink away,
We will drain the cellars out
If those worthy men should gain the day,
And Bastard kept out,
And Bastard kept out, my boys.

When the Votes were ready for to start,
It was a pleasant thing
To hear the band so sweetly play,
And Black Torrington's bells to ring;
To see the ladies in the place
Walking up and down
Taking their farewell of these loyal Votes,
As they marched out of the town, my boys,
As they marched out of the town.

We'll drink a health to Parson Coham,
And merry will we be,
And wish him health and happiness,
And all his family.
And now we'll push the beer about,
With cheerful hearts we'll sing -
Success attend those worthy men,
God save the King and Queen,
God save the King and Queen!

Lord Ebrington came top of the poll, with Sir Thomas Acland a close second.

The Pack Horse Inn, licensed to sell beer and cider, was owned in 1843 by Richard Hockin. Richard was the elder brother of William and, like his father Abraham, was a cooper. They probably worked for William Chapman the local maltster. Richard died in 1854 and Richard's widow, also Elizabeth, continued at the Pack Horse for a few years before retiring and going to live with her daughter, Fanny Hutchings, in West Chilla. By 1878 the Pack Horse had changed its name to become the Commercial Hotel. Shadrack Stacey was the innkeeper in the 1880s, during which time his wife, Thirza, bore him three daughters. In 1890 he took over the licence of the Clovelly Arms in Bratton Clovelly and Richard Brock became the last landlord of the Commercial, for after a short time he relinquished the licence and the premises became a private dwelling.

The two village inns were known in the Victorian era as the Higher Pub and the Lower Pub. Their residential guests were mostly travellers who came to country shops and tradesmen who hoped to gain orders for supplies – be it groceries, clothing, hardware or building materials. These inns were the meeting places for at least two clubs in the nineteenth century according to the memory of the late Laura Luxton (who died in 1999 aged 97). There was the Women's Club, known as the Fourth of June Club, which went to the inns in turn for its annual mid-day dinner. Members marched to the church carrying flower-decked banners for a thanksgiving service. There were sweet stalls in front of the Union Hotel and dancing in the street or in Centernhay, and sometimes in the gardens of The Larches and The Rectory, to music from accordion and fiddles. In 1909 the school was given a holiday on June 21st and 22nd for the 'Club Festival'.

Christina Hole in her book "English Custom and Usage" suggests that many of these village clubs inherited the customs of the old Whitsun Ales which were held at this time of year, consisting of a church service, procession, dancing and games.

There was also a Young Tradesman's Club established in 1836 at the Union Inn. This was a club to provide for relief in times of sickness and the local doctor was its medical officer. The first of these was Dr Rudall who appears to have lived in Black Torrington in the 1830s until 1839 when he moved to Sheepwash. He was a paid-up member of the club but received an annual fee for his services. In 1850, when Dr Owen opened a practice in Black Torrington, he was medical officer but was not a club member.

From 1842 to 1878 there were between twenty-one and thirty members belonging to the Young Tradesman's Club. They paid 12/- (60p) for a year's subscription (later 14/-). Sickness benefit was 8/- a week for 'lie beds' and 4/- for 'walking'. £6 was paid for a funeral, £3 for women. They held six meetings a year with an annual meeting on 30th May with dinner at 1/6 a head (7¹/₂p). The club paid 2/- for beer at ordinary meetings and 10/- at the dinner. In 1878 the Club's fund of £200 was disbursed among the 29 members in ratio to length of membership. Although they called themselves 'young' there seemed to be no age limit and many continued their membership for thirty or more years. Most villages had similar Friendly Societies or Associations, such as the Foresters at Sheepwash, and some still have their annual parades, as at Iddesleigh. Many of them ceased after the passing of the National Insurance Act in 1911.

The Union Hotel continued in the twentieth century, firstly managed by Samuel Broad and then, from 1918–1953, by John and Jack Beare who ran it for the People's Refreshment House Association. For much of this time the Beares ran an annual horticultural show; at first in the field next to the inn (the present car park) and then in the Public Hall. The Coham estate sold the inn in 1953 and the new owners ran it as a free house. In 1962, when F.E.Broadhurst was landlord, the name was changed to the 'Torridge Inn', and in the 1970s the small public bar was enlarged by removing the central passage and incorporating the sitting room. In 1978 the building was enlarged with a public games room added, only to be reduced in 1999 when the addition was converted into a separate dwelling.

Union Hotel decorated for the Coronation, June 1911 (also Club Day).

DOCTORS

The earliest reference to a doctor in Black Torrington is 1827 when Thomas K. Tapley Esq., surgeon, of Black Torrington married Mary Hearn of Shellhouse, Shebbear. The following year their daughter was baptized at the parish church. Robert Rudall, surgeon, was living in the village when his two children were baptized in 1835 and 1837. He appears to have moved to Sheepwash in 1839.

Dr Arthur Willoughby Owen was the first doctor to practise from The Larches and the first to establish a regular surgery. He was an Exeter man who trained in London as a surgeon and apothecary. His name appears in the Black Torrington list of *White's Directory*, 1850, as 'Owen, surgeon', indicating he was newly arrived. At first he lodged with William Chapman at Long Hall. In 1851 he had lodgings at Cuckingstool with Emanuel Horn, but when the Misses Peacock vacated the New House in the Square in 1856 (which they had rented from the Burdon estate) Dr Owen moved into this house, later named The Larches. In the 1861 census he is listed as living near the Rectory assisted by his 15 year old nephew, James Sadler. They were served in the house by Harriet Creper, a 35 year old widow from Clawton. Dr Owen stayed in the village for some 30 years. By 1881 he had been joined by his elder brother John, also a surgeon, from Middlesex, who was remembered by Henry Bailey for playing the violin.

Several doctors followed in quick succession: there were five between 1886 and 1903 (see Appendix 7).

In 1903 Dr George Candler arrived in Black Torrington. He had trained at St. Thomas' Hospital and was medical officer at a tea estate in Assam for a few years before coming to Devon at the age of 32. He married Edith Benedicta Whistler, a relation (possibly niece) of the painter, James Whistler. She herself painted in both oils and water-colours and worked in wood, leaving a carved mantle shelf and oak panel in The Larches. Dr Candler served in the R.A.M.C. in the first World War, when he was attached to the Royal North Devon Hussars. While he was away his patients had to attend the surgery at Shebbear. He was a keen horseman, riding to visit many of his patients as well

Dr. George Candler c. 1920

as riding to hounds; he kept his horses in the stables opposite the house. He retired in 1929 to live in Bradford. He died in 1940 and was buried in Black Torrington where a memorial to him was placed in the church. His two immediate successors, Drs. Worsley and Michael, stayed only for a short time.

Dr Richard Gordon Gwynne came to The Larches in 1933 at the age of 31, and newly married. He was an Australian from Adelaide and trained at the London Hospital. He was soon accepted by the Devonians and devoted his life to their welfare. He was medical officer for Winsford Cottage Hospital and public vaccinator for Black Torrington and Bradford parishes. It was during his time, in 1948, that the advent of the National Health Service completely changed the practice of rural medicine. No longer would his patients settle their accounts when they were able, and often in kind – a brace of pheasant or a sack of potatoes – (the poorest never being charged) but for the first time there was free treatment for all and an assured income for the doctor. Dr Gwynne became a much loved and respected doctor and friend, ready to visit at all times of day and night, even if this entailed walking across fields or trudging through snow to isolated farms and cottages. When he died in 1971 he was still in practice after 38 years. A memorial fund was set up in his memory and the Dr Gwynne Trust was formed which in 28 years has donated over

£2000 to medical research and to help equip the local medical practice. The Larches stayed in the possession of his family so after more than 110 years it ceased to be 'the doctor's house'.

His successor, Dr Roger Filer Cooper, did not live in the parish but had a surgery built in the village that has been a great benefit for all. At first the surgery was held at Karinya in Mr and Mrs Bryant's sitting room, then at Coham Bridge House and then in a caravan on the new surgery site beside the old people's bungalows in Bowhay. This temporary surgery was first used in July 1972. Initially there was difficulty in obtaining planning permission for a two-story building, and on account of access, so a petition of support was circulated in the neighbouring parishes that attracted over 1,000 signatures. Blake House was completed in May 1974 and formally opened by Peter Mills, M.P. in August. Dr Filer Cooper retired in 1990 and was succeeded by another doctor from overseas: Dr Asad Al-Doori. He came from Iraq to Edinburgh to complete his medical training and stayed as a political exile. Like his two predecessors he was quickly assimilated into the community, and will long be remembered for his courageous work in preventing the sale of Winsford Cottage Hospital and thereby saving it for the use of the community. The parish is very fortunate to have been served so well for so long by its medical practitioners.

Broad Street in c.1913. Mary Blight, parish midwife on right.

The pump in The Larches wall with Joy Perkins (standing) and Margaret Chapman 1932

SCHOOLS

Of the private school, mentioned in the Visitation return of 1798, we know nothing. In 1836 the rector, John Penleaze, and churchwardens petitioned the Bishop of Exeter for permission to build a school in the churchyard alongside its southern entrance, after a vestry meeting agreed to the need and desirability for a parochial school. A faculty was granted on 28th October, giving control to the Rector, and the school was built with the aid of a Parliamentary grant. By 1841 John Braund was the schoolmaster at the age of 34 years. Whether he was the first master is not known. He was born in Milton Damerel and stayed at Black Torrington for possibly 40 years. He remained a bachelor living in lodgings in the village. The school was enlarged (substantially rebuilt) in 1875 at the cost of £260. This sum was largely raised by public subscription. The leading subscribers being Mr Bickford Coham and Mr. W.A. Saunders (who owned Forda with 750 acres), the National Society, Mr. Thomas Fisher, the lord of the manor, and Mr. Penleaze, the rector. The architect was Samuel Hooper of Hatherleigh, the mason was Frederick Chapman and the carpenter was Emanuel Horn. The first master of the new school was Mr George Passmore, with his wife as sewing mistress, but he stayed for only eighteen months. In 1877 the schoolmaster was Exeter-born Garth Chapple, then aged 23 years. By study of the 1881 census it would appear that he was living in Porch House with his young wife, Emily. Mr Chapple appointed Miss Mary Gilbert (daughter of the late James Gilbert the auctioneer) to be an assistant mistress, but the managers dismissed her in 1880 when she failed to satisfy the inspectors. She set up a rival school in the cottage now named The Briary, but this did not last very many years. The headmaster from 1882 was Samuel Penwarden, from Holsworthy, who was only 18 years old when he came and not fully certificated. With him came his elder sister, Elizabeth, as sewing mistress. The school log book for 1883 reports low attendance due to an outbreak of diphtheria. The average attendance in 1883 was 55, although there were about 70 pupils on the register. Compulsory attendance existed in theory but did not become the norm in rural schools until the turn of the century. In 1890 Mr Penwarden went to

Sutcombe School where he stayed many years. His sister stayed a further year before marrying George Denford, the shoemaker, who had been for several years a widower.

In 1892 Her Majesty's Inspectors of Schools demanded that an infant classroom be built. As a result the school was extended in 1894, when a further faculty was given to enclose another piece of the churchyard to the north to lengthen the main classroom by some 8 feet, and to enlarge the porch entrance. For the autumn term of 1894 the infant children were taught in the chapel Sunday School room. Here, unknown to HMI, the children had to use an open field as a latrine! The architect this time was Lucius Reichel, who was also a keen antiquarian and horticulturist and had bought and restored the old farmhouse at Beara about ten years previously. The cost of the school extension was £185, most of it being borne by the new rector, Mr. Jephson Gardiner.

In the same year Mr. Reichel drew up plans for a new one-roomed school at Chilla to accommodate 36 scholars. There had been an earlier school at Chilla whose master, in 1870, was Plymouth-born John Mills. The school was condemned in 1893 as dilapidated and unsatisfactory. The building was 'disgraceful, dirty and unfit for teaching children'. John Mills married, as his second wife, Emily the daughter of Thomas Luxton. They are both buried in the graveyard at Chilla Chapel. The new school was opened in 1895. At the turn of the century there were 30 children attending and the master was William G. Jones. In November 1951 the school was closed and converted into a private house named 'Chestnuts'. All the children were sent to Black Torrington village school.

In 1849 John Daw, of East Budleigh, bequeathed to the churchwardens a house and garden in Broad Street called Porch House with directions that, after keeping the premises in good repair, the rent be applied to maintain a schoolmaster or mistress. Although this was done by his son and heir there was no conveyance and in 1872 the Charity Commission made a scheme under which the clear annual income, after payment of proper outgoings and expenses, should be applied to support a Sunday School. Porch House, which was originally two cottages (one very small) was rebuilt in 1876 by public subscription at a cost of £205. Messrs Chapman and Horn, who built the new school in 1875, were employed in the building. For a number of years the house came to be known as School House, but reverted to Porch House in 1982.

In 1890 Robert Mills, probably the son of John Mills of Chilla (both were born in Stonehouse), succeeded Mr Penwarden. His wife, Sarah, bore him three children who were baptized at the parish church between 1892 and 1895. In 1893 the school was closed for one week, by Dr Spencer, because of an epidemic of catarrh. The average attendance was 65 and Miss Laura Chapell was the infant mistress. In 1894 the school was given a holiday when the room was required for a tea given by Dr. Spencer on the occasion of his marriage.

2/ £68.10.0   Black Torrington
                August 7. 1875

Received of the Reverend John
Penleaze the sum of Sixty Eight
Pounds ten Shillings being my
share of a Contract entered into the
sixth day of April 1875 for Carpenter's
work in rebuilding the School Room

                Emanuel Horn

1/   Black Torrington
                September 18, 1875

Received of the Reverend John
Penleaze the Sum of One hundred
and forty two Pounds sixteen Shillings
Masons Work in Building the new
School Room

                F J Chapman

Contract — 135
Extras   7 16
          £142 16

Receipts for the re-building of the School, 1875

Earliest known photograph of Black Torrington School, taken in the old playground c. 1896-7. Headmaster, Mr Robert Mills. Fourth from right in the front row is Maggie Hobbs.

A School Group outside the Rectory barn c. 1900 with Mrs C Mitchell, extreme right.

School Infant class 1915: Mrs Mitchell right; Nellie Born left.
Back row: 2nd from left is Alfred Jury; far right is Cecil Chapman
Centre row: 1st left Jack Wooldridge; 2nd left Clarence Fry; 4th left Cecil Moast; far right is Willie Isaac
Front row: 2nd left is Marcia Down; 4th left is Catherine Dennis; 5th left is Ivy Chapman

School Group 1929. Headmaster Mr LJ Stanbury.
Back row: Reg Baily, Ron Baily, Harold Hunkin, Bill Slade, Sidney Chapman.
Centre row: Claud Baily, Archie Luxton, Molly Weavon, Dolly Winser, Margaret Smith,
Phyllis Isaac, Joyce Bray, Audrey Keast, Jim Richards, Percy Winser
Front row: John Parsons, Gwen Chapman, Ethel Martin, Kit Winser, Pam Baily,
Teresa Copplestone, Roy Luxton, Leslie Cleverdon.

School Group c. 1948. l to r. Back row : Melina Winser, Mary Jury, Pauline Moast, Jacqueline Dart, Betty Chapman, Esther Jones, Dora Wivell, Sylvia Willis, Stella Martin, Fay Luxton.
3rd row : Mrs Stenlake (teacher) Fernley Jones, Frank Martin, Derek Smale, Courtenay Dart, Dawn Winser, Ann Winser, Mary Hollands, Rachel Jury, Pat Stratton, Maurice Down, Ralph Chapman, George Davey, Bernard Smale, Mr Tom Glasson, Headmaster 1937-51 (absent, at war 1940-45).
2nd row : Lorna Jones, John Ivey, Ken Jones, Russell Laughton, Sylvia Dymond, Joan Langman, Priscilla Yelland, Ann Langman, Desmond Ley, Leslie Hunkin,   ?   .
Front row : Raymond Martin,   ?   , Brian Stenlake, Bill Langman, Jean Stenlake, Phyllis Ley, Margaret Lashbrook, Pam Barkwill, Reg Barkwill, Peter Hunkin, Albert Winser.

School Sports in Playing Field July 1958. Mrs Gwynne presenting Cup to Elizabeth Knight & Trevor Hill. (Brewery Cottage still standing in the background beside the Public Hall).

Lewis Tonna Dibdin Doctor of Civil Law OFFICIAL PRINCIPAL OF THE EPISCOPAL CONSISTORIAL COURT OF *Exeter* lawfully constituted, To all and singular Rectors, Vicars, and Curates lawfully appointed, within the Diocese of *Exeter* but more especially to the REVEREND *John Samuel Jephson Gardiner* Clerk, *Rector* of the *Rectory* and Parish Church of *Black Torrington* in the County of *Devon* and Diocese of *Exeter* Greeting. Whereas the said *John Samuel Jephson Gardiner* and the CHURCHWARDENS of the said Parish of *Black Torrington* have by their PETITION humbly prayed the Right Reverend the Lord Bishop of *Exeter* for a faculty for erecting on the churchyard of the said Parish of Black Torrington on the site indicated by the plan thereto annexed an extension of the Parish School-room which was in or about the year 1836 erected on a portion of the said churchyard under a faculty from the said Lord Bishops Predecessor dated 28th October 1836 such extension being made necessary by the requirements of the Education Department who had approved of the proposed site and extension and no graves or tombstones would be interfered with by the said extension.

Faculty application for the School extension in 1894

Maypole Dance in the School's new playground c. 1963

The School bell was given in 1898 by Mr James Sparke, and in 1900 Dr Whitelaw closed the school in July due to an outbreak of measles. In the same year the school inspector said that a better means of cleaning slates must be provided "without having recourse to the mouth and sleeve". In December 1915 the school had many absentees because of whooping cough and in May 1917 the school was closed again, for three weeks, because of an epidemic of measles. Mr Mills left at the end of 1902 for Ivy House School, Broadwood Widger.

Thomas Wheadon was appointed head master in 1904; he too had children baptized during his headship (two between 1908 and 1911) and lived at Long Hall. The infant mistress was Mrs Caroline Mitchell, who had been appointed in 1896, and stayed until 1917. The average attendance was slowly increasing, and in 1906 it was 72. The school log at this time refers to regular holidays and half-holidays granted for national and parish events, particularly for Church and Chapel teas and fetes, and in September 1918 two half-holidays for blackberry picking! There were whole day holidays in 1922 and '23 for the weddings of Princess Mary and the Duke of York. The log also records the extremes of temperatures: in July 1911 it reached 82° Fahrenheit, and in February 1917 it was only 27°! Mr F.T.Eastwick succeeded Mr Wheadon in 1912 but on 2nd July 1915 he wrote, "My duties as Head Master cease from today until the end of the war." In fact he did not return, and in 1920 John William Heard was appointed. In 1923 Mr Heard had two assistant teachers: Miss Ward and Miss White. Leslie Stanbury was the schoolmaster from 1926-1930, and in the 1930s Miss Frances Chapman (grand daughter of 'gentleman Joe' Chapman) was an assistant mistress.

In 1937 Mr Glasson, from Lyme Regis, was appointed headmaster and was joined by Miss Dorothy Stephens from Mary Tavy, who was at the school from 1938 to 1942 when she married George Chapman of Upcott. During the war the school numbers were increased by some 60 children who were evacuated from London (in 1939 attendance had dropped to 45). Most of the evacuees arrived on 16th June 1940, together with four teachers. The Public Hall and reading room provided additional classrooms. Altogether 98 children between the ages of 5 and 14 were taken in by fifty homes in the parish (29 children were in Chilla and went to Chilla School). Mr Marshall Down, the parish clerk, acted as billeting officer (his daughter, Mrs Barbara Pett, possesses his log book, and kindly made it available). Nearly twenty of the children had returned to London within 6 months, and half had returned to their homes by the end of 1942. Some 30 children stayed for the duration of the war, and some still return to visit their war-time homes. Mrs Joan Trengove, who became assistant mistress in 1970, and stayed for 20 years until her retirement, had herself been an evacuee during the war in neighbouring Sheepwash.

In 1940 Mr Glasson joined the R.A.F., returning to school after the end of the war, in 1946, and staying until he left for Willand in 1951, the term before the children from Chilla came to the village school. During the war the children played their part in 'digging for victory', the Rector letting them use part of his garden (now the garden of Wistaria) and the glebe field adjoining. The school had very primitive lavatories – seats over an open drain that was flushed once a day - and a very small playground. The children would play in the lane outside the rectory barn. Discussion continued for several years in the 1950s as to how to resolve the latter shortcoming. Numbers of children attending the school were severely reduced in 1948 when all those over 11 years were sent to Hatherleigh school, and by 1950 there was talk of the school being closed because attendance was down to 22 children. In 1953 the school was designated a Church of England Voluntary Controlled School and the local Education Authority became responsible for the maintenance of the buildings, while the Church retained the right to appoint two managers. In 1957 the Rector conveyed the rectory barn and the land behind it (which was part of his glebe land) to the education authority, these were then re-conveyed to the rector in his capacity as school trustee. This gave the school a hall and a playground. In the same year a new kitchen was built so that school meals could be cooked on the premises (cooked meals had first been brought out from Holsworthy in 1943). The school kitchen was closed in December 1980 by the County Education Authority as an economy measure and meals were distributed from Ashwater. The kitchen was "moth-balled" for a while in case of a change of policy but eventually the cooking facilities were removed.

The 1980 Education Act changed the name of the 'School Managers' to 'Governors' and a new Instrument of government was issued in 1982. The barn unfortunately deteriorated over a period of 45 years and had to be demolished in 1999. A new classroom, library and office were built on the site in 2000.

Several masters succeeded Mr Glasson (see Appendix 6) but none of them stayed very long. In 1970 Mr Rourke was appointed. He was the last head teacher to live in the village, at 1, Sparke Villas, which was then owned by the County Council. It had been purchased as a Constabulary house in 1925 and when the last policeman left in 1965 it was let to the incoming headmaster, Mr Bruce Hall. Jim Rourke died in 1983 at the early age of 55 years. In 1968 a pre-school play group was started, meeting on two mornings a week in the school barn: this was continued for 30 years.

*Eliza Bright, newsagent, with Harry Seaward 1926.
Billboard reads "Devon Drug Smuggling Allegations".*

CRIME AND THE POLICE

The earliest record of crime in Black Torrington is noted in the burial register with the burial of Elizabeth Badge in March 1746/7. It is annotated with a margin note that reads: "a Child wilfully murder'd according to the jury's verdict by a Person or Persons unknown". Elizabeth was the daughter of John and Mary Badge, baptized in January 1738/9.

The county constabulary was established in 1839. The earliest evidence of a policeman living in the village comes from the baptism records for 1859, when Edwin the son of John Adams, police constable, was baptized. Robert Tarring, police officer, had two children baptized in 1871 and 1874. He probably lived at the cottage now called Kite Cottage. This is the Constabulary House where Samuel Kite lived for some years after 1900. He had five sons baptized between 1901 and 1906.

In 1907 there was a shooting on the Chilla road. Two young women, Alice Ivey and Maud Slade were walking home to Higher and Lower Graddon on a Sunday evening in February after attending Chilla chapel; they were accompanied by Alice's two younger sisters. As they neared Fraunch gate they were passed by 21 year old Robert Lamble, who lived with his grand parents at Ley Court. Shortly afterwards a shot was fired: the girls, who were terror-struck, screamed and ran. Maud and one of the younger girls ran on, while Alice and her sister ran back. Both the older girls had been sprayed with gunshot. Robert Lamble came from behind the hedge and struck Maud in the back with a knife. Mr Slade was waiting for his daughter at Graddon Cross, and he ran down the road and, meeting the two girls, took them to Mr Ivey at Higher Graddon. Meanwhile Alice was overtaken by her assailant at Fraunch gate (Park View had not been built at that date) where he attacked her with a knife and the butt of his gun and left her as she collapsed unconscious. When she recovered she was alone and began to stagger homewards until she was met by her father and Mr Slade. It was by then nearly 10 o'clock. Dr Candler was called, and P.C. Kite, who was on duty outside the Union Hotel, received the news and proceeded to Graddon on his bicycle. From there he went with

PC Kite with his wife outside the Constabulary house c. 1904

William Ivey and George Slade, the injured girls' brothers, together with Fred Ball from Fraunch, to Ley farm where Mr Lamble, senior, came down from bed and let constable Kite into the kitchen. There his grandson, unknown to him, was sitting with the gun. P.C. Kite pushed the gun aside as it was fired and the shot went into the wall. The constable grappled with his assailant and handcuffed him. He was taken to Holsworthy Police Station and in the morning was charged with shooting at P.C. Kite with intent to murder.

Apparently Robert Lamble had wanted to court Miss Ivey, but was not encouraged. He did not appear to understand the gravity of his action. Maud Slade was not seriously injured. Miss Ivey had wounds to her head and neck, but soon recovered.

The last constable to live in Kite cottage was Harry Chilcott who moved from there to The Villas (i.e. 1 Sparke Villas, which was built with No. 2 in the 1880s by James Sparke) in 1925. Later in the same year Albert Winser was appointed to Black Torrington and lived at the Villas for ten years until his retirement, when he moved to Devonia. In 1949 Frederick Pearce was constable when there was a disturbance at Coham, which was then being run as an hotel. One of the guests, Tom Ogden, had quarrelled and had gone out into the grounds with a gun. The police were called and P.C. Pearce asked Dr Gwynne to go with him. They found Mr Ogden, a 32 year old former naval man, in the grounds of Coham. Fred Pearce struggled with him and was struck a heavy blow on the head. The policeman drew his truncheon and, in endeavouring to make Ogden drop the gun (which was later found to be unloaded), hit him on the head with fatal consequences. Tom Ogden died in hospital and the inquest jury returned a verdict of justifiable homicide.

None of the constables after 1935 stayed very long – there were ten in thirty years – the last being Michael Bate who left Black Torrington in 1965 and the parish was then policed from Halwill, and later from Holsworthy.

There were also Special Constables in the parish. Both Jim Knight and Claude Blight were active in the 1960s.

Samuel Hunkin Harris beside the Black Maria built at his carriage works bearing the Newcastle-Upon-Tyne coat of arms, c. 1905

John Avery Organ built 1791, restored 1988
Memorial to John D. Burdon on right.

photo © Tony Freeman Press Agency

THE CHURCH (1790-2000)

As was noted earlier the Revd. Richard Warwick Bampfylde, who graduated from Brasenose College, Oxford, in 1781, became Rector in 1783; the Revd. William Holland Coham was his curate, and effectively the parish minister, from 1790 until his death in 1825. In September 1797 a vestry meeting agreed that a 12 penny church rate be made for the purpose of 'erecting a new pulpit, reading desks and seats and partitioning off part of the church for a vestry room and other purposes, for which a faculty had been lately sought'. Those attending the vestry were W.H. Coham, J.D. Burdon and J. Chapman (churchwardens), James Hearn, Richard and James Paige, Anthony Tucker, Richard Balsdon and Elias Leach. The new seating caused several disputes as some parishioners found their accustomed places had been removed, and some others who had subscribed for the new seating had to be accommodated. In June 1799 Mr Coham and the churchwardens submitted to the Bishop's court in Exeter 'an allotment of sittings' in the church. Another vestry meeting held on 31st December agreed that the north wall of the church, being very ruinous, should be repaired with new windows; and a further church rate be collected by the churchwardens. Two twelve penny rates brought in £85.2s. Richard Stettaford was paid £63 as a first installment for the new seating. Of this work in furnishing the church only the sounding board above the pulpit remains today. The windows for the north wall were not new: in 1798 the representatives of the late Lord Clinton were paid £2.5s. for two stone windows, which were brought from the old mansion of Heanton Satchville in Petrockstowe which had been burnt down. The following year Joseph Chapman was paid 2s.6p. for the expense of going with a horse to 'Henton' to fetch the stone for the windows.

The Exeter Flying Post reported that on Thursday, 29th November, 1798, the Rev'd William Holland Coham, M.A., curate of Black Torrington, preached to the Black Torrington Corps of Volunteers on the day appointed for General Thanksgiving. This was for Nelson's victory over the French in the Battle of the Nile. In that year the Devon Militia records state that John D. Burdon Esq.

was officer of the Black Torrington Infantry. In 1803 James Hearn and Anthony Tucker are both recorded as being members of the Sheepwash Troop of the North Devon Yeomanry.

In 1819 another faculty was granted for building a gallery, or loft, in the north transept for the choir with five seats each side of a central passage; underneath there was to be similar seating and space for a vestry. A pew for the tenants of the Coham estates was to be placed in front to the west of the pulpit. The subscription list for this work in 1820 was headed by Richard Bampfylde, the rector, William Arundell Harris, the lord of the manor, and William Holland Coham, the curate: each gave £10. Stephen Coham gave £5, as did Mr Leach, but he was paying for exclusive right to a pew. Joseph Chapman gave £3 for the same purpose. In 1827 a new altar-piece was erected. John Davidson (who wrote notes on many Devon churches in the 1840s) describes an altar screen of painted wood with fluted pilasters and urns. There were constant references in the churchwardens accounts, from the end of the 18th century, to payments for musical instruments - a bass viol, a tenor viol, a German flute, a clarinet, a violin cello, singing books - and in 1804 payment was made for teaching the art of singing psalms, spiritual songs and anthems. In 1842, £4.1s. was spent on a choir dinner. The gallery was removed in 1869; in which year a harmonium was purchased and the musicians became redundant. There was another gallery at the west end of the nave which is mentioned by John Davidson in 1849. This was removed in 1872 and the tower was opened. At the same date encaustic tiles were laid in the chancel.

There were continual admonishments to the Rector and churchwardens from successive Rural Deans for the repair of the Rectory house from 1811 to 1822. It was declared to be ruinous and in a disgraceful state, and in need of re-building. In 1821 Mr Bampfylde wrote that the rectory house "is so old I am going to build it new". In 1826 Mr Bampfylde and Mr W.B.Coham were both present for Archdeacon Froude's Visitation on 19th September. The altar rails and the chancel floor are reported as needing repair but nothing is said about the house so it had presumably been rebuilt, or was rebuilding, by then. Throughout these years repeated mention is made of the nuisance of pigs in the churchyard, as well as horses and geese! In fact reports of gaps in the churchyard hedge continue to be made until almost the end of the century, and are not unknown even today. In 1821 the Revd. W.H.Coham was receiving a stipend of £82.10s. and fees for serving as curate. The return for that year gives the number of communicants as 50 (four times a year). Sunday services were at 10 a.m., with sermon, and at 2.30 p.m. Before the death of Mr. Coham in 1825 his eldest son, William Bickford Coham, became the parish curate with a stipend of £42 p.a. His mother was the heiress of Dunsland and it was there that he lived.

Richard Bampfylde died on 15th September 1834, aged 75 years. His brother was Sir Charles Warwick Bampfylde, who had been Member of Parliament for Exeter and was assassinated in 1823. He was shot by the husband of one of his servants, who then turned the pistol on himself. Sir Charles was taken to his London home and died a few days later, not from the bullet wound itself, but by infection from the copper wire of his braces which had been carried into the wound with the shot. Richard's nephew, George, succeeded to the baronetcy and was created Baron Poltimore in 1831. The advowson (the right to present a new incumbent to the Rectory) had been purchased from the Bampfyldes, sometime before 1834, by John Storey Penleaze, who was a barrister and one time M.P. for Southampton. He presented his younger son, John Penleaze, a young graduate from Oxford who had been made deacon in 1832 and had spent two years as curate in Hereford. He was instituted on 30th September, only 15 days after the death of Mr Bampfylde, and inducted into possession of the freehold in October. He came to a nearly new rectory as its first permanent resident at the age of 25.

The date of John Penleaze' marriage is not known, but his wife, Elizabeth Alethea, bore him a daughter, Emily, who was baptized in October 1839. A son was born two years later but he lived only 15 weeks. In 1869 Emily married the Revd. Samuel Andrew, Vicar of Halwill. After 13 years Mr and Mrs Penleaze vacated the rectory, presumably to journey abroad, and the parish was left in the care of a curate, Westcott Veale, who lived at the rectory for 12 years. Mr Veale, a bachelor, was the son of James Veale of Passaford in Hatherleigh. Westcott Veale became Vicar of Hatherleigh in 1862 but died the following year.

In 1851 a religious census was compiled for England and Wales. The return for the parish church was made by James Gilbert, the parish clerk. He estimated the number of seats in the church as 350, with 150 free. It is hard to imagine how 350 people could have sat comfortably. His figures for attendance on 30th March are 200 in the morning and 100 in the afternoon, with an average of 200. Perhaps all the figures are somewhat inflated. The number attending Sunday School was given as 60.

In 1861, soon after the Penleaze family returned to Black Torrington Rectory, a handsome gift of silver was made to the parish by Mr Holland Coham (younger brother of the Revd William Bickford Coham). This consisted of a chalice, paten, flagon and plate which have the hallmarks of Martin Hall of Sheffield, 1860. The vestry meeting agreed that the old Georgian chalice should be sold and another one bought to match the new one. But in the end Mr Coham paid for the chalice and paten to be restored and they remain in the possession of the Church. This silver was made either by John Burdon or John Babbage in Exeter in 1740. Holland Coham was a scholar and a lifelong cripple. He lived for many years at Dunsland spending most of his time in the library, according to Bickford Dickinson in "The Dunsland Saga".

Shortly afterwards another gift to the Church was made by Arscott Coham, a solicitor in Holsworthy, in memory of his parents, William Bickford and Augusta Mary Davie Coham. This was a new stained glass window above the altar, depicting the Resurrection, which was made by Lavers, Barraud and Westlake in London in 1869, and was erected in 1870. The following year Mr Penleaze installed a stained glass window in the tower, and in 1876 a window at the west end of the south aisle in memory of his wife, Alethea, who died in June 1875 at The Rectory. Soon another memorial window was to be erected next to the last. John Penleaze died at The Rectory in June 1879 and parishioners subscribed to a window in his memory. In 1875 another gift was made to the church by Miss Mary Coham in consequence of an incident many years before. Her brother Stephen, a midshipman in the navy, was leaving the village one day to rejoin his ship when he stopped to ask Hugh Balkwill the time of day. Mr Balkwill obliged, adding, "as far as I can gather from our old clock". To which the young Stephen Coham replied, "If I ever live to come back again I will fix a good clock in the tower". Sadly he was drowned soon after, at the age of 22, by the upsetting of a boat near Deal, and returned only to be buried on 13th November 1819. Presumably Miss Coham left directions in her will, for she died in Plymouth in January 1875. The clock, made by Gillett and Bland, was placed in the tower later that year. It has two faces: one on the south facing the village and one on the west facing Coham.

The advowson seems to have reverted to the Bampfyldes as the next rector was presented by the 2nd Baron Poltimore and was inducted by the Revd. J.R.Powell of Buckland Filleigh on 21st December 1879. This was John Russell, one of the so-called 'hunting parsons', popularly known as 'Jack Russell the Sporting Parson'. John Russell was born at Dartmouth. After education at Blundell's School and Exeter College, Oxford, he was licensed as curate of South Molton and later became curate for his father at Iddesleigh. In 1833 he was appointed to the Perpetual Curacy of Swimbridge in North Devon. When Lord Poltimore offered him the living of Black Torrington he was loath to leave Swimbridge, but the stipend there was little more than £200 and he was finding it difficult to live within his means. Black Torrington's endowment would give him a clear £500 a year. He wrote, "How can I leave my own people with whom I have lived in peace and happiness for half a century? It will be a bitter pill to swallow. . . but it will be my poverty, and not my will, that will consent to it." On leaving Swimbridge he received a handsome testimonial amounting to nearly £800. This was presented to him by Earl Fortescue who said it was a mark of their regard and respect "for Mr Russell as a man, a sportsman and a clergyman."

Although John Russell was already 83 when he came to Black Torrington he was still hunting regularly with both stag and fox hounds. He built new stables at his own expense opposite the rectory where now Wistaria Cottage stands. Tragically within hours of this being completed the stables burnt

Black Torrington (1882)

18th Jan.y 1882 —
My dear Mrs Hartnoll —
    Since Dec.r the 21st — 8 o'clock in the morning I have received at least 140 congratulatory letters on my attaining "unto" my 86th birthday, but no one has sent me a more pleasing contribution, or one that I value higher than I do yours —
Thank you, thank you very much for it, & for your kind re-collection of my natal day, & all the good wishes express'd on your pretty card —
    I am, as I know you will be pleased to hear, getting a little more reconciled to my new home — but then it is not, & never will be Swimbridge to me — but yet my neighbours & Parishioners do all they can to make me feel happy here, & I am becoming so — thanks to a very great degree to my dear little Mary, who is always most kind & attentive to me, and has won golden opinions among all — great & small — of my friends & neighbours — There are some large landed proprietors with good houses in the neigh-bourhood, but they reside here only a few months in the year — spend the others in London, & this place becomes desolate accordingly, but I have some 8 or 10 couple of Harriers, & plenty of Hares, & neighbours around me who love the sport, so I am not very miserable! Remember me, please, in the kindest man-ner to all your family — Mr & Mrs Sloorke, John & his wife included, & believe me
    Your's very sincerely
    J. Russell —

Letter written by Parson Jack Russell from Black Torrington to Mrs Hartnoll of Swimbridge.

The Revd. Jack Russell with his dogs c 1870

The Rectory
Black Torrington
23rd March — 1883 —

My dear Loveband —

altho' the cheque for 25 which I drew on you yesterday will "all but" square all my tradesmens Bills & servants wages up to Lady Day — next Sunday — still I think you had better send the order for the usual sum, in case I should see, & wish to purchase a good? estate on Broadbury!!! & I will sign, & return it by return of post — I haven't been outside the door since last Saturday — My kindest regards to you both —

Yrs very sincerely
J. Russell

Mr Loveband Esq
Bank — Torrington

Previously unpublished letter from Jack Russell, a month before his death, to his bank manager.

down, two horses and two terriers perishing in the blaze. It must be stated that Parson Russell did not hunt to the detriment of his pastoral duties. At Swimbridge he increased the Sunday services from one to four. He loved children and soon after he arrived in Black Torrington (according to an article in Bailey's Magazine) he gave a tea for 200 of them – church and chapel – and gave each child a little present. In 1881 John Russell took the evening service at Buckland Filleigh. The Western Times reported that 'he drew far more than the church would hold – many came from a distance, and were much delighted with the reverend and venerable gentleman's address, equally attractive to royalty as to yeomen.'

The tale of the notice on the church door reading, "Evensong at six if the fox is caught: if not, not" is somewhat apocryphal, especially as hunting does not take place on Sundays. However Mr Russell would think nothing of hacking 20 miles to a meet, hunting all day and then riding 20 miles home again. He was at Black Torrington for only four years, though during that time he entertained the Prince of Wales at the Rectory at least once: villagers were said to report that 'Mr Prince' was at the Rectory.

The 'Jack Russell' terrier that he bred was a much bigger dog than those commonly seen today. Its height was 14 inches and a dog would weigh between 16 and 18 pounds. Its coat was thick and short and it was bred to go to ground to bolt the fox and not to kill it. Russell was a member of the Kennel club which he joined in 1873 and he did some show judging, but he gave it up because he thought that a terrier had a job of work to do and show dogs became too valuable to be worked. John Russell died at the Rectory on 28th April 1883. He was buried at Swimbridge where at least a thousand people attended his funeral: poor cottagers brought baskets and aprons full of flowers and these were showered on his grave.

The Devonian Russell was followed by an Irishman, John Jephson Gardiner: he was born in 1845 and was a graduate of Trinity College, Dublin. He came as a widower with an eleven year old son, and in 1885 he married, in Plymouth, his second wife, Clara Jane Wood. In that year a new lectern was presented to the church in memory of her father, Charles Wood, who had died in 1884. By the evidence of the books he left behind Mr Gardiner was something of a high churchman but he is chiefly remembered for his building work. Although he is recorded as speaking at the Archdeacon's Visitation at Holsworthy in 1902 when there was a resolution against the publication of betting news in the daily press. He pointed out that "gambling often went on in the harness rooms among gentlemen's grooms when they drove their masters out for the evening." In 1896 Lucius Hurlock Reichal of Beara Court became churchwarden, and continued in that office until 1909. He was an architect by profession. He had already been active in the building of the school and Porch House; now the Rector engaged him in planning the restoration of the church. In 1884 Mr Gardiner had set about improving the lighting

The Revd. Jephson Gardiner with his wife Clara and son John.

in the church, with three brass coronas, each to hold twelve candles. He also instigated repairs to the tower. In 1890 the necessity for a general restoration was recognized and by 1897 plans were being drawn up and a faculty was applied for to re-build the chancel, re-organize the seating and move the vestry from the transept to its present position at the east end of the south aisle. Bishop Bickersteth wrote to Mr Gardiner wishing "that every blessing will rest on the great and good work" and added, "I am sure that your own example in re-building the chancel yourself will stimulate the members of your flock, and also your friends and neighbours".

The local restoration committee reported that the church was in a deplorable state: roofs leaky, walls bulging, square pews with rotten boarding over the vaults beneath, fine old carved oak wagon roof (south aisle) obscured by plaster which was falling down. The committee advised that the Revd Medley Fulford, who had supervised the restoration of North Lew and Pyworthy churches, should be appointed consulting architect in addition to Mr Reichal, who gave his services. There was one contentious matter to be decided: whether the new roofing should be Delabole slate or Brosely tile? The tiles were favoured on account of their durability. Four contractors tendered for the work; Mr Grant of Torrington was successful. The nave was to have a new oak roof (to be copied from the previous one) which would extend the whole length of the church, and the chancel was to be widened and lengthened with a new north window. The floor was to be laid with marble: black and white in the chancel and red Devon marble in the sanctuary: this would replace the encaustic tiles which had been laid in 1872. The floor of the nave was to be lowered and paved with maplewood blocks. Part of a Norman piscina, or holy water stoup, was found during the work and was inserted in the east wall of the transept. A carved head was also found in one of the walls and was placed inside the south porch. Over the porch a new cross of Halwill stone was erected. The upper part of the arcade between the nave and south aisle was pushed back to make it vertical, and buttresses were added to the south wall. Among those who worked on the restoration were Aubrey Born, carpenter, Walter John Chapman (the first), mason, and James Smale.

The re-opening service was held in July 1903. The Bishop of Crediton preached a 'powerful' sermon. Mr Clotworthy of Launceston was organist for the occasion, though the Western Times reported that "the music was not what would be expected on such an eventful occasion. The hymns were sung too rapidly and without any respect for the consideration of the Non-conformists who are not accustomed to the Establishment service." The church was elaborately decorated and afterwards there was a tea in the schoolroom. The cost was over £2000 (the original estimates were £1100). The Gardiner family contributed over £600 for the work in the chancel. The subscription list was headed by the curate, Edward Donaldson, with 100 guineas. He also presented a new organ – or rather an old organ, as it was built by John Avery in

*Restoration of the Church, 1900. On the right is Lucius Reichel, architect and churchwarden.
On the left Jim Smale. Photo taken from the north-east.*

Wedding of Frederick Born and Rhoda Jury, Long Cross, 2nd April 1902. Revd. J Gardiner seated left.

Club Day The Rectory June 1909

London in 1791 and was purchased from Berrow church in Somerset. Mr J. Risdon, Mrs. Andrew (presumably the daughter of Mr Penleaze) and Miss Clarke of Macclesfield each gave £100. Mrs. Coham gave 50 guineas. Mr Blyth Coham-Fleming, her son-in-law, gave £50 as did Mr James Sparke, of Smithsland, who had been churchwarden from 1874-1896.

Miss Beryl Kelly was the regular organist; she had played the harmonium since 1885, and continued as organist until 1923. She was succeeded by Miss Edie Dart who had an even longer career (although not continuously), retiring in 1973.

Hard upon the re-building of the church Mr Gardiner set about enlarging the Rectory by adding a new east wing in 1904. In 1905 a 'superior heating apparatus' was installed in the church (a system of pipes which are still used today), and in the same year some substantial oak pews were placed in the nave. The pew bench ends in the nave were carved by Col. E. Woodward Scott, of Torrington, in 1927.

Edward Donaldson, who became curate in 1900, was appointed rector of Pyworthy in 1904. Mr Gardiner soon found another curate, a Cambridge graduate from a Somerset family, Mr Thomas Buncombe, aged 45. Three years later, in July 1907, Mr Gardiner died at the age of 62. Mr Buncombe succeeded, being presented by Mrs. Gardiner. Two years later a new pulpit, carved by John Northcott of Ashwater in the Jacobean style, was erected in memory of the late Rector. The pulpit was said to be modelled on one in Liskeard and was dedicated by the Bishop of Crediton. At the same time the old oak sounding board over the pulpit was taken down, cleaned and varnished and re-erected. In 1909 new oil lamps were introduced to light the church in place of candles. In 1911 Mrs Gardiner gave a new altar table and reredos, also carved by John Northcott, in memory jointly of her husband and her mother. The former altar was placed in the north transept, and also a wooden screen was erected across the tower opening. Clara Gardiner died in February 1911. The following year there was to be a memorial to Clara herself, given by her sister, Madeleine Frazer: this was a sedilia (triple seat) placed on the north side of the sanctuary.

In 1920 Mr and Mrs Henry Beal of Bridge Farm gave a litany desk in memory of their son George Cutland Beal who was killed in action at Bapaume, during the first battle of the Somme, on 18th October 1916 whilst serving as a gunner with the 4th Worcester Regiment. In the same year a memorial plaque to all those from the parish who died in the 1914-18 war was placed in the north transept. In 1957 it was refurbished and the additional names of those who died in the 1939-45 war were added.

The Diocesan return from Black Torrington for 1919 records 120 names on the electoral roll (first introduced in that year) but only 60 communicants. There were 10 members on the Church Council, 5 Sunday School teachers, 40 scholars, 16 choristers and 12 bell-ringers. The day school had three teachers

*Six Bells to be re-hung 1924. On the left Harry Seaward and Harry Ham.
On the right Edgar Chapman and Albert Saunders*

*The Church Choir 1959. Back row Ernest Broad, Miss Dart (organist), Bernard Ham, Dorothy Chapman.
Centre row: Jeanette Baily, Sheila Willis, Heather Kivell, Evelyn Chapman,
Nora Chapman, Vera Winser, and Barbara Lock.
Front row : Stephen Chapman, Jeremy Smith, David Willis, William Thomas, Fred Sillifant, Michael Ivey, Jason Smith, Velma Millman and Revd. Courtney Johns.*

and 80 pupils. Church expenses amounted to £20 for the year, £10 was given to the poor and sick of the parish, £7.5s. to Home Missions and £4.16s. to overseas Missions.

In 1923 the bell frame was reported in bad condition, and the following year the six bells were re-hung on a cast-iron frame on steel girders; new clappers were provided and the bells 1/8th turned. The work was done by Messrs Gillett and Johnstone of Croydon for £300 which was paid for by donations. This was the year in which Stephen Balkwill died. He had been church sexton for thirty years, dying at the age of 87. The rector's wife, Mrs Annie Buncombe, died in 1927. Her daughter, Helen, continued to live with her father at The Rectory until he died in 1941, aged 82. Miss Buncombe led the Girl Guides who used to meet at The Rectory, where the Mothers' Union also held their meetings. The Black Torrington branch was in existence from 1908 until 1987. In 1935 the church was lit by electricity.

Thomas Buncombe was a member of the Royal Horticultural Society from whom he received the Bar Medal for the propagation of the daffodil, of which there were rare varieties in the Rectory garden. For his last four years Mr Buncombe was assisted by a curate: first Evan (Taffy) Hitchings, from 1937-39, and then Ronald Adkins from 1939-41. Mr Adkins was later Rector of South Pool, near Kingsbridge. Dr Arthur Gardiner presented the Revd Frank Dossetor to the living in 1941. In 1943 Mr Dossetor left the parish for three years to serve as an army chaplain, and Mr Hunt was curate-in-charge until 1946, when he was appointed Vicar of Frithelstock.

The Revd Percival Comeau followed Mr Dossetor in 1949. He had been in Plymouth throughout the war and his church of St Saviour, Lambhay Hill, was destroyed in the air raids. His son, Maurice, became rector of the neighbouring parishes of Bradford and Thornbury in 1951. In 1956 George Copplestone died. He had been churchwarden for 31 years, and his family gave a carved oak bishop's chair to the Church in his memory. Another long serving churchwarden, John Jury, died in 1967. He was elected in 1928, and served for 39 years. The longest serving warden was George Smale Risdon who was warden for a total of 42 years between 1821 and 1883, though not continuously.

In 1973 the three parishes, of Black Torrington, Bradford and Thornbury, were formed into an united benefice with the Revd Ronald Baker as Rector. A new rectory was built in Black Torrington in the orchard of the old rectory, which was sold. Mr Baker moved from Bradford Rectory into the new house in 1977. Within a year he moved and the author became the occupant of the new rectory for the next twelve years. On 16th June 1974 lightning struck the south-east pinnacle of the tower ten minutes before Evensong on the Sunday afternoon. Five choir members and the organist were in the vestry. Fortunately due the heavy rain no other members of the congregation had arrived as some debris fell into the nave, though the bulk of the pinnacle came

*'Topping Out' August 1974, after the tower pinnacle was struck by lightning.
Revd. RH Baker leading the toast.*

to rest in the roof valley. The Rector had sagaciously delegated the conduct of Evensong to a Reader on that Sunday and was himself safe in the Rectory at Bradford! The pinnacle was salvaged and restored and the church made safe within two months, during which time the services were held in the school barn. An earlier lightning strike had dislodged the south-west pinnacle during the war in the 1940s, but it fell away from the building, narrowly missing the Gardiner memorial below the tower. After the second strike a lightning conductor was fitted.

The benefice was increased with the addition of Highampton in 1982. In 1989 the Avery organ was restored and repositioned to face west (instead of north into the choir stalls). The work was supervised by William Drake, of Buckfastleigh, at a cost of £9,000. The church clock was converted to an electric winding system in 1996. Another £9,000 was spent in 1998 refurbishing and conserving four of the monuments in the church; one memorial to Benoni Bampfylde, one to Anne Hearn and two to the Coham family.

Black Torrington Rectory 1977

Old Buildings in the Rectory yard, 1955, before it became the School playgound

Chilla School at Bethel Cottage – c.1890.
Emily Mills (Mistress), John Mills (Master).
Top row: Nellie Muired, Ada Down, Bessie Wooldridge, Mary Wooldridge,
Bessie Blight, Elizabeth Dart, Nellie Horrell.
Middle: Jessie Clarke, Carrie Blight, Lenny Down, Mary Jewell, Laura Hill, Laura Down, Jessie Knight.
Front row: Mary Horrell, Lizzie Jewell, Charlie Mills, Minnie Pyke.

CHAPELS

There are no dissenting chapels recorded in the returns for Black Torrington before the 19th century. When the Revd. William Holland Coham completed the Bishop's Visitation return as curate of the parish in 1821 he wrote that there were 'dissenters... but of what sect it is uncertain. There is a meeting-house now building but none as yet licensed' (although in 1809 a licence had been issued for a meeting room in Joseph Bailey's house). Roger Thorne, the Methodist historian, has suggested that this would have been a Baptist meeting for the Baptist records list a chapel in Black Torrington in 1823, when the pastor was John Metters. There was a building in Back Lane marked on the 1843 tithe map as a Methodist chapel on land belonging to Joseph Chapman, indicating that the Baptists had not flourished here. In the 1830s James Hunkin of Black Torrington, formerly a champion wrestler, was, with his brother, 'brought to the Lord' and became a Baptist. John and James were the eldest sons of Samuel Hunkin of Buckpitt. James was a friend of Alex Facey who was minister at a chapel built on the Facey's farm at Muckworthy in Ashwater. James emigrated to the U.S.A. in 1836. Two younger brothers, Jonas and Robert, also went to America. Another Black Torrington Baptist was George Maynard who had ministerial oversight of the Ashwater Baptist church for nine years: he also ministered at Hatherleigh. Mr Maynard, who came from North Lew, lived in Highampton for a while and later farmed at Hope Farm. His daughter Clara married John Pellew in 1894. A Baptist chapel was established in Sheepwash before 1835.

The chapel in lower Back Lane, near the site of Fox's Orchard, was possibly used as a temporary measure by the Bible Christians, who became a separate denomination from the Wesleyan Methodists in the early nineteenth century. They owe their origins to the preaching of William O'Bryan, and one of their earliest centres was at Lake in Shebbear. In 1843 the Bible Christians were building a new chapel at the top of Bonfire Hill in Black Torrington on land again belonging to Joseph Chapman. A deed was made on 31st March between Joseph Chapman the elder, and James Damrell and 14 others, for a piece of ground 'in a field called Broom Park. . . for a Bible Christian Chapel'. The chapel was given the name Hope, and in 1851 John Ward was the steward, who in the religious census of that year estimated that the average attendance was 100. He gave the number of sittings as about 70, with 30 of them being free. There was standing room for 120, and there were about 30 Sunday School scholars. In 1865 the chapel was enlarged, and in 1873 a deed was made between Edmund Chapman and John Chapman and 8 others for an additional piece of ground to enlarge the burial ground. The chapel was restored in 1885 at a cost of £160, and rebuilt in 1921. On 1st August 1910 the Black Torrington and Sheepwash Gospel Total Temperance Society held their annual meeting with a parade through the village led by the Hatherleigh United Methodist Temperance Brass Band. There followed a service in the chapel at which Miss Dufty played the organ, and afterwards there was tea in the adjoining schoolroom. The president, Mr A.Chapman was unable to be present through indisposition.

The present chapel had a grand opening on Thursday 12th May 1921. Several hundreds gathered just after 11 a.m. when the Revd. H.E.Reed introduced Mrs. Down of Barnstaple who opened the doors. Morning service followed when the Revd. J.Ford Reed delivered 'an eloquent and impassioned sermon'. Luncheon was held in a large marquee close to the new chapel: Mr R.N.Stranger of Tavistock presided. There followed a concert in the Day School by the Torrington Orpheus Choir. So many wished to attend that it had to be repeated later in the day. This was followed by a sale of gifts, conducted without charge by Messrs Calloway & Co. Sheep, lambs, poultry, goats, pig and dead stock were offered and the sale raised £133.18s. Several hundred went to the tent for tea (the report in the Shebbear Circuit Magazine says 'upwards of a thousand people') which was given by Mr and Mrs Wooldridge. There were too many people for the chapel to hold for the evening service which was presided over by the Revd. W.B. Reed, so an overflow meeting was chaired by the Revd. P.W. Luxton. The cost of the new building, including the acetylene lighting installed by Mr Bright of Merton, was £1,400. On the following Sunday Miss Abbott, who shared the position of organist with Mrs Wooldridge, received a presentation to mark the occasion of her forthcoming marriage.

The earliest Bible Christian chapel built in the parish was in the Western Hamlet, part of Bradford at Holemoor. This was Rehoboth chapel built in 1839. White's Directory for 1850 states that there were both Baptist and Bible Christian chapels in the village, so perhaps the Back Lane chapel continued as a Baptist chapel for a while after the building of Hope Chapel.

There were Methodists meeting in a farmstead in East Chilla in 1816. Perhaps this was where William O'Bryan preached when he came to Black Torrington on 30th March 1816. In 1840 a Bible Christian Chapel was built on a site adjacent to the present Chilla House and named Emmanuel. In 1848 the

The old Hope Chapel before 1920
(an enlargement from a vignette)

Sunday school treasurer was John Hunkin. It is possible that it was the Sunday school of this chapel that was the first Chilla day school. In 1851 the chapel steward was Richard Squance and the average Sunday attendance was reckoned at 90. The trustees in 1871 were John Smale, William Yelland, Benjamin Hopper, Daniel Hutchings, Richard Luxton and Thomas Down. In 1889 a presentation was made to Mrs. Hopper in recognition of her playing the harmonium. In 1892 a new chapel was built on the corner of the new road to West Chilla on ground bought from David Clarke, until lately the lord of the manor, and in 1898 a graveyard was opened. The new trustees included Messrs Hopper, Hutchings and Luxton together with James Luxton of Westlake, William Hutchings and William Clarke (all farmers in Chilla) and James Knight of Hole Farm; also William Wooldridge who farmed at Henderbarrow, Albert Down, a Chilla blacksmith, James Down, a shoemaker from Halwill and William Chapman, a signalman at Halwill Junction.

Chilla Chapel was included in the North Lew circuit; Holemoor (Rehoboth) and Black Torrington (Hope) chapels were in the Shebbear circuit. All three chapels continued in use throughout the 20th century. The nearest Wesleyan chapels were at New Inn, Shebbear and Brandis Corner in Bradford. Both these buildings have been converted into domestic dwellings. In 1871 Richard Hawkey, a Bible Christian minister, lodged with Stephen and Ann Vanstone in a cottage on Bonfire Hill near to Hope Chapel. He was, presumably, the assistant minister in the Shebbear circuit for the manse is in Shebbear.

Sheepwash Foresters in Black Torrington, May 1908.
(The two cottages below the shop were still thatched).

Club Day c.1910. Led by Mrs Fanny Hutchings, local Registrar, and Mr & Mrs Isaac. On the left Florrie Balkwill, Mary Blight and Mrs Harris followed by the flag and the band.

CHARITIES

Much has already been written about the Churchlands Trust (see page 41). It is now regulated by a scheme ordered by the Charity Commissioners in 1885. The ex-officio trustees are the Rector and Churchwardens for the time being, and up to six other nominated trustees, who together may use the income for the maintenance and repair of the fabric of the parish church, and for the maintenance of the services and the furniture. Another charity already mentioned is John Daw's Gift, made in his will of 1849 (see "Schools"). The Charity Commissioners order was not made until 1873, which appointed the Rector and Churchwardens as trustees to use the clear annual income for the support of a Parochial Sunday School. Mention has also already been made of the Dr Gwynne Trust (see "Doctors").

Further charities were established under the wills of John Risdon and Eliza Tucker. John Risdon died at Stourbridge in Worcestershire in September 1913 and left £1000 to the Rector and Churchwardens to be invested; half to be used to keep the parish churchyard in proper and decent order (with any surplus to support a parish nurse), and the other half to provide "suitable clothing or blankets or other necessaries to such of the aged or infirm or deserving poor persons as they shall think fit". Mr Risdon also left part of his library and several pictures to the village Reading Room. John Risdon was the third son of George Smale Risdon of Hayne. George Risdon came to farm Hayne and Blackley in the early 19th century from Buckland Filleigh, and died at Hayne in 1889 at the age of 93. A brass alms dish and two collection plates were given to the church in memory of George and Susanna Risdon by their children. John's elder brother, Edwin, was nominated a Churchlands trustee in 1885, continuing until his death in 1909. James, the youngest and last of the Risdons of Hayne died in 1921.

In 1933 Eliza Tucker died at Sparke Villas, where she had lived for over 40 years. Aged 84 she was the last surviving daughter of Anthony Cornish Tucker of Totleigh Barton. She left £1000 to the Rector of Black Torrington to be invested: half the income was for the poor of Black Torrington annually at

Christmas; one quarter was to go towards the expenses of the annual outing of the choir of the parish church, and the last quarter towards an annual treat for the scholars of the parish school. In 1968 the Charity Commissioners amended the scheme for the poor in line with John Risdon's (i.e. need, hardship or necessity).

Another charity for the poor was provided by Peter Speccott of Thornbury Manor who died in 1655. By his will he left £180 to be invested in land for the benefit of the poor of Black Torrington and Holsworthy, with which a cottage and 16 acres of land were purchased. This land is situated between Highweek and Blackley, part of the holding of Ley. Four ninths of the income was to be applied for the benefit of the poor of Black Torrington or "of such deserving and necessitous persons resident therein". The other five ninths was for the poor of Holsworthy. The Charity Commissioners approved the present scheme in 1891, revised in 1902. The Black Torrington trustees comprise two trustees appointed by the parish council and five co-optative trustees from persons residing, or carrying on business, in or near to Black Torrington. In 1891 the representative trustees were Mr L. Reichel and Mr William Sparke; the co-optative trustees were the Revd. Jephson Gardiner, Mr Blyth Coham-Fleming, Mr Richard Balsdon, Mr James Risdon and Mr James Sparke.

Finally among the parish charities is the Newcombe Charity which resulted from a bequest made in 1912 by William F. Newcombe of Cleveland, Ohio, for the poor of his birthplace (he was born at Smithsland in 1826). There was some delay because his will was challenged, but eventually in 1915 a sum was invested in £923 War Loan.

Miss Mabel Beal decorated for twenty years' service to the National Savings Movement, May 1962 Left to right: Mrs Marshal Down, Mr Veale, Mrs V Smith, Mrs Alfred Down, Mrs Doreen Ivey, Miss Mabel Beal (Mrs Jeffery and Miss Dart, behind), Mrs Moast, Mrs Nellie Hunkin, Mr Hollaway, Miss Nora Chapman, Mrs Holmes

PARISH COUNCIL

Parish Councils were formed throughout England and Wales in 1894, and were the lowest rung of local government under the District and County Councils. They took over some of the functions of the old vestry meetings that had appointed overseers for the poor and for the highways. The civil administration of the Western Hamlet (Middlecot) and the Eastern Hamlet (Totleigh) had passed to Bradford and Highampton parishes respectively in 1884 (although the ecclesiastical parish boundaries did not change until 1929).

Black Torrington was allotted nine councillors and in December 1894 there were 21 candidates. Those elected were: David Balsdon, farmer, South Trew; Henry Beal, farmer, Bridge; Aubrey Born, joiner, Frederick J. Chapman, sub postmaster; William Clarke, farmer, West Chilla; William S. Isaac, butcher, The Poplars; Charles Jenn, gentleman (also a local Baptist preacher), Kingsley House; James Edwin Vanstone, machinist, Devonia; and Henry Ward, mason. They held their first meeting on 31st December 1894, when Henry Beal was elected chairman (he continued in this office until 1919), Jimmy Ned Vanstone was elected vice-chairman, and the schoolmaster, Robert Mills, was elected clerk at a salary of £2.10s. (this was reduced to £2. in 1896).

Daniel Balsdon stayed on the Council only two years, and Lewis Perkin, contractor, of Gorford, took his place; he himself only served two years and John Pellew, farmer, of Hope Cottage became a councillor in 1898. There were no contested elections between 1894 and 1907. Mr Isaac served the longest, 34 years, being chairman from 1919-1928. In the early years four sub committees were formed: allotment, charity, finance (W.S. Isaac was elected treasurer in 1898) and cottage garden show. The first cottage garden show was held in 1898, but it is not certain how long the shows continued. In 1901 Aubrey Born stood down and John Bailey, a tailor of Bonfire Hill, took his place.

Matters which occurred most frequently in the early years related to local foot-paths: for instance the style into Centernhay field, for which the Rector was asked to provide a gate, and the footbridge to Buckpitt, which Mr Coham-Fleming was asked to renew. There was much concern about the village pumps and wells. There was a well at Kingsley cottage, a well below Gorford (to which a pump was added in 1920) and another (with a pump) opposite the Public Hall and one beside Rose Cottage opposite the hall car park. There was a pump in The Larches wall opposite the present entrance to the playing field, and one next to Centernhay Cottage (opposite The Stores). Other wells were at the top of Bonfire Hill, one further down at Long Cross, one in Back Lane, near Fox's Orchard, and one opposite Kneela. Many houses and cottages had their own private wells either in the house or in the garden.

The village roads also occupied the Council's time. The Council tried to get Back Lane from Venn to Long Cross adopted by the County Council in 1897, but without success. The lane leading off to Butterbear and Smithsland was in even worse condition. The postal service was given attention with requests for collection boxes to be provided at Ducking Stool and at Chilla, and the maintenance of Sunday deliveries was also pressed. Allotments, street-lamps, roadside walls and sanitation were also discussed as well as the appointment of trustees to Speccott's charity. For the first four years the Council meetings were monthly (although there was not always a quorum). In 1898 bi-monthly meetings were adopted.

Robert Mills left the parish in 1902 and James Bawden Born was elected clerk. Mr Born was the younger son of Robert Born who came to Black Torrington in the 1840s with his farming father and set up as a butcher after his marriage to Gertrude Bawden in 1860. Aubrey the carpenter (councillor from 1894-1901) was his elder brother and lived at Rose Cottage (now Coram House), and his eldest brother, Richard, farmed at Buckpit. James, a tailor, married Edith Chapman in 1892. Edith helped to run the post office at Broompark cottage, next to the Methodist church, for her father, Frederick, who combined the job of sub postmaster with his work as a mason. Her sister, Mary, took over the post office when their father died in 1905. James resigned as parish clerk in 1919 when he became sub postmaster, and was elected to the Parish Council in the same year. James Born later became registrar for the Black Torrington sub district and held all these offices, and that of churchwarden from 1929, until his death in 1936.

In 1898 the Council resolved that the parish became one of the local centres for technical education, and asked for classes in 'ambulance' and 'ploughing' to be arranged. In 1903/4 the subjects were to be 'bee-keeping', 'laundry' and 'dressmaking'. In the 20th century roads and footpaths continued to be a concern, including the road to Fishleigh and the condition of Buddle Lane to Smithland. The parish pumps continue to feature and the street-lamps, which had been maintained by Mr James Sparke of Smithland. In 1903 he died and in 1904 (when Mr. Garret Jones, headmaster of Chilla School, had taken Mr Chapman's seat) the following resolution was passed: "the Council unanimously desire to express their condolence with Mrs. Sparke on the death of her beloved husband and to place on the records of the Council the high

Looking north from the Chapel 1903. Post Office on right. Cottage on left later rebuilt as Hamilton House.

*Gardening and bee-keeping class at Hope Farm 1904.
Extreme right Lewis Dart, centre with back to camera is 'Gentleman Joe' Chapman.
On the left wearing cape is Mrs Vanstone.*

appreciation held by the parishioners of all classes and creeds of the late Mr James Sparke's goodness of character. He invariably bestowed his munificence to the advancement of schemes that have greatly contributed to the better well-being of the community, religiously, educationally and socially. The Council especially record the help he pecuniarily gave in sustaining the parochial schools in a state of efficiency, to the securing of a water supply, and the lighting of the village for public benefit".

In the autumn of 1904 the Council engaged Mr J.B.Born to light the village lamps for the winter, agreeing to pay him £4. These were acetylene lamps burning carbide and were to be lit half an hour after lighting-up time for vehicles, from 27th October until 25th March. He was to omit the four nights before the full moon and the four after each full moon. Repeatedly for several years parish meetings were called to consider whether the cost of lighting should be on the parish rate or by voluntary subscription. A vote to put it on the rates was always defeated. The last village lamp-lighter was John Moast.

About this time the Council was asked to pay 6d. a year to the lord of the manor as an acknowledgement for the pumps in The Larches wall and opposite the Supply Stores. After a year of correspondence and debate they agreed to pay 3d, only to be told (on paying the account) that payment should have been made by the District Council. Other items on the agenda at this time were the appointment of a school manager and the question of whether to support a district nurse for the parishes of Black Torrington, Halwill and Ashwater. This item was deferred and did not appear again until 1915! By the end of the war a parish nurse was appointed - Miss Hilda Pope.

In 1907 there were 19 candidates and a poll was demanded, which cost the parish £8.5s. As a result three members lost their seats: Mr Jenn, John Bailey and Mr Garrett Jones. The new councillors were John Hopper, farmer of West Chilla, John Jury, carpenter of Bonfire Hill and James Risdon, farmer of Hayne, who was elected vice-chairman. The new council resolved that its meetings would be quarterly. In June 1908 it was reported that people were taking water from the village pumps for other than domestic purposes. It was resolved that they be locked at certain times because of the shortage of water. (This occurred again in 1928). The following year the Council agreed to support Shebbear Parish Council's appeal for the extension of the railway line from Great Torrington to Halwill. After the war in 1919 this call was renewed, particularly as "it would take heavy traffic off many miles of road". Mr Born was given a new contract to light the village lamps for the six winter months until 31st March for £6. In 1912 George Copplestone, who had taken over the butcher's shop from Mr Isaac, was co-opted to the Council in place of Henry Ward. Mr Copplestone served on the Council for 44 years, and was Chairman from 1936-46.

In 1919 there was an election and Richard Baily, of Highweek, John Isaac, son of W.S. Isaac, and James Born were elected in place of Henry Beal, James Vanstone and John Hopper (who had left the parish). Mr Beal had been chairman throughout his 25 years on the Council. W.S. Isaac (who had moved to Butterbear) was elected chairman, and John Jury became vice chairman. The post of clerk was advertised at a salary of £16 a year and Mr Lewis Dart of Torridge House was chosen. The office was re-advertised the following year and Mr Marshall Down was appointed with a salary of £20 a year. This rate of pay did not last very long. By 1927 the clerk's salary was £3.5s. and in 1959 it was raised to £8. Mr Down was parish clerk until his death in 1963 - a service of 43 years. In 1960 the Council presented him with a table lamp to commemorate forty years of public service. George Chapman succeeded him, resigning his seat as councillor: he served for six years and was presented with an eight day clock on his retirement in recognition of public service over a period of 40 years – councillor from 1929-34 and 1949-63, and clerk from 1963-69. Mrs Ruth Luxton, who had been elected a councillor in 1967, likewise resigned her seat and was appointed clerk at a salary of £15. In 1973 inquiry was made as to the appropriate rates of pay for a part-time parish clerk, and it was discovered that the minimum rate was £37! Since then the salary has followed national guidelines, and Mrs Luxton continues as clerk. There have been only six parish clerks in 106 years.

In 1919 a parish meeting was called to discuss the building of a public memorial to those who fell in the war. A tablet, or a cross, with a drinking fountain was favoured, to record 'deep gratitude to all those who had, at the call of duty, given their services in defence of Liberty and Honour'. Estimates were to be obtained and a site chosen, either opposite the Union Hotel or opposite the village Stores. In 1921 the latter ground, given by Mr Bickford Coham-Fleming, was conveyed to the Council and the Memorial erected. In July 1919 the parish celebrated the signing of Peace with a united service of worship, a free tea and sports, for which councillors canvassed subscriptions.

In 1922 there was another election, and Richard Hutchings, who was farming Buckpit, took the place of J. A. Isaac. This was reversed in another election six years later when there were 21 candidates and Mr Hutchings and Samuel Wivell from Forda lost their seats to John Isaac and Ernest Chapman. The Council reverted to bi-monthly meetings until 1940 when it again only met quarterly until 1964. Throughout this time the condition of the wells, their occasional pollution, and the repair of the pumps took much of the Council's time, as well as correspondence with the Charity commissioners and appointment of trustees for Speccott's and Newcombe's Charities. The state of the back roads and the danger at Windmilland Cross were discussed.

The North Devon Railway, connecting Torrington with Halwill Junction, finally came to Black Torrington in 1924. Hole lane leading to the new station needed improvement; this was accomplished using stone from Woodhill quarry. The Council was disappointed that the station was named "Hole", rather than "Black Torrington". In 1963 the Council protested against the threat to close the railway from Torrington to Halwill, but to no avail, and the line was closed in 1964.

There was a request for a public telephone in the village in 1923. There is no record of when it was provided but in 1938 the Council requested that a light be provided within the kiosk (repeating the request in 1949).

In 1924 the Council again requested Holsworthy District Council to take over the road from Venn Cross to Long Cross (Back Lane). This was refused until the road was put in good order. This took a long time and the road was not adopted until after the war. There was a similar case with the road from the village to Highweek.

The need for a refuse dump was discussed in 1928 and it was suggested the disused quarry by Black Torrington Bridge might provide a suitable site. In 1929, it was agreed to rent this from Mr Coham-Fleming and to fence it. Even after the introduction of the District Council collection, indiscriminate scattering of rubbish was a problem that persisted, some people continuing to use the old site even until 1977. It was cleared and closed in 1979.

There were continual problems with sewers, which were piped though Crabhay (known as Kelly's Meadow) and Town Meadow (The Maltings), under Back Lane into an open stream which ran down to the River Torridge. In 1926 the sewer pipes were reported to be in a bad way. In 1929 the Council sought ways of getting a better water supply and improving the sewer system. With the building of the Public Hall in 1930 the sewer in Mr Chapman's field (Town Meadow) had to be reconstructed, and in 1931, 70ft of new pipe was laid under the road at the bottom of Kneela hill, although there was still an open ditch through the meadow. In 1934 the inadequacies of the water supply were again discussed, and in 1937 the sewer drain from the Villas was reported to be broken and polluting two wells. In 1959 a new sewer was laid from the School along East Street to a new sewage treatment works opposite the old quarry (refuse) site. In 1980 the sewer connections from Broad Street through the playing field were in a poor condition and in 1987 South West Water accepted responsibility for the repair. The work was put out to tender, and effected somewhat shoddily; it was not until 1990 that it was properly completed and the gardens re-instated.

In 1934 the West Devon Electric Supply Co. brought electricity to the village and in 1938 the Council inquired about the possibility of electric street lighting. This was discussed regularly at Council and Parish meetings from that date until 1970. The problem was that the cost would fall upon the local ratepayers and was thought to be too much. In 1959 the members of the Women's Institute petitioned the Council for street-lamps, but it was rejected at a parish meeting by 83 votes to 34. The solution came when the charge was no longer on the local rates and was absorbed in the county rate. In 1971 lights

*George Chapman with his
son Stephen at Upcott
1957.*

*John Jury in the farmyard,
Long Cross
1957.*

were placed in Broad Street, East Street and Victoria Road (East Street appears to have been named in the mid 19th century and Victoria 'Lane' is mentioned in 1912). In 1974 the Council agreed to reduce the lighting because of a national power shortage: every alternate light was turned off and the Council said there was no need for any lighting in the mornings. Not until the 1980s were extra lights added, in Back Lane and Long Cross and on the road down to the River Torridge. In 1992 'all night' lighting was introduced at the request of the Council.

The war in 1939 put an end to further hopes for an improved water supply. In 1947 there seemed to be no prospect of a mains water supply and a bore hole was sunk in the field below Ducking Stool, water being piped to a reservoir above Upcott. In 1949 there were complaints about the state of the roads which had been dug up for pipe-laying. At last the village pumps became redundant except for those at Gorford and Long Cross. This remained the water supply until about 1970 when pipes were laid from Prewley to bring water from Dartmoor. During the drought of 1976 consideration was given to re-opening the bore to avoid having to depend on stand pipes, but the supply was condemned as unfit for drinking.

There were 14 nominations for election to the Parish Council in 1931 but none of the existing councillors were unseated. After this there does not appear to have been another contested election until 1946. During the war the Council was involved with the billeting of evacuees, air raid precautions and collections to help the war effort. In 1952 Miss Daphne Coham-Fleming, Mr Brian Down, Mr Michael Isaac and Mr Cecil Moast were elected in place of James Knight, William Slade, John Dunford and Herbert Chapman. Miss Coham-Fleming was the first woman to be elected councillor. In 1973 she stood down from the Council and Dr Roger Filer Cooper became a councillor (one of only 6 nominations). A secondary election was held in July when there were seven candidates. Messrs Colin Kivell, Clifford Baily and Stanley Baily were elected to the three vacant places. Dr Filer Cooper was elected chairman and it was agreed that notice of agenda be sent to councillors before meetings and that a summary of the proceedings should be sent to the local press. But it was not until 1991 that the minutes of meetings were published. In 1974 the Council met monthly, but in 1975 reverted to bi-monthly meetings. There was an election in 1979, and the last contested election was in 1991.

Highway problems continued to occupy the attention of the Parish Council in the second half of the 20th century. In 1954 the Devon County Council was asked to provide a speed limit through the village; this was a problem which was to be raised many times. In 1966 the Council wrote to the Member of Parliament (for Tavistock) to enlist his help in the matter. All this to no avail: the speed limit was not introduced until 1985. Long Cross, Windmilland Cross and Hope bends were all considered dangerous. Part of the hedge was removed south of Long Cross in 1979 and the bank cut back at Windmilland

Oli Down working on railway cutting, Hole Station, 1924.

Unveiling of the War Memorial 1921. Miss Louisa Chapman on the left and Mr Jim Knight in the foreground.

in 1993. Improvement at Hope was not achieved until 2000. In 1955 there were complaints to the Council about cars being left parked in the village street. This problem was first mentioned in 1930! In 1962 and 1972 attempts were made to find an area for a village car park. A part of Centernhay field opposite the Stores was identified but the plan was not proceeded with; it was raised again in 1976 and the Council paid for plans to be made and entered into discussion with the Diocese of Exeter with a view to purchase, but nothing was achieved. The possibility of providing a car park in Centernhay was discussed again in 1991, but residents in Broad Street said they would prefer to park outside their houses. Space for car parking outside the council houses was provided in 1983. The Council had speedier action over its complaint to the Rural District Council about the flooding of the houses in Broad Street caused by the raising of the road level due to resurfacing. The complaint was made in April 1960, repeated in October 1961 and by November 1962 a high kerb had been laid along the edge of the pavement!

The desirability of building council houses in the village was proposed in 1931 and discussed regularly in the following years. In 1938 the Council requested the Rural District Council to build six houses for 'the agricultural population'. Sites were considered at East Chilla, Upcott hill and on Higher Lane (the road to Highampton). In 1939 two further sites were considered: the two and a half-acre field at Bowhay and a field at Windmilland. Then came war and in 1947 planning regulations were introduced. It was not until 1951 that Bowhay was identified as a definite site and the first pair of houses was built (numbers 5 and 6). Two more pairs were built in 1952. In 1963 the two pairs of bungalows designed for elderly people were built on the western edge of the field. In 1971 a request to build more houses or bungalows fell on deaf ears, and in 1973 the District Council sold off the rest of the site, part for the new surgery and the rest as three private building plots.

The Parish Council built a bus shelter on the edge of the playing field in 1956 after complaints about school children having to wait in all weather with no shelter before catching the school bus to Holsworthy. The public conveniences were built in 1971 and are maintained by the District Council.

Local Government was re-organized in 1974. Holsworthy Rural district was swallowed up in Torridge district, and in 1975 Black Torrington was joined with Sheepwash and Shebbear to form a voting district for County and District councillors. In 1890 Joseph Chapman and Edwin Risdon served on the Holsworthy Rural district council, and in the 20th century those who served were A.J. Isaac, John Pellew, E. Wooldridge, E.C. Ham, J.A. Isaac, A. Chapman, G. Copplestone, and B. Down. In 1975 proposals were made to change the parish boundary, and in 1992 all the houses on the main road to the east of South and North Trew were transferred to Highampton.

In 1974 Mr Tovey, who had bought Harry's Meadow (formerly Town Meadow) from Harry Chapman in 1963, obtained planning permission for nine dwellings to be built there (4 houses and 5 bungalows). The site was sold to Fontbeam Construction who, in 1982, varied the application to build 2 houses and 7 bungalows. In 1988 the site was cleared and Maltsters Hill widened, but the building fervour subsided in 1989 and Fontbeam went into liquidation. The site remained an eyesore until a new builder started the development in 1997. Additional land to the south provided room for four more dwellings and planning for these was approved in 1999. Other recent building developments were two bungalows built in 1975 adjacent to Briary Cottage, two bungalows south of the chapel yard in 1977 and two bungalows opposite these on Bonfire Hill in 1982. The bungalows in Victoria Road, with the exception of Gardenia, were built spasmodically over a long period between 1968 and 1991.

In 1953 the Council planned to celebrate the coronation of Queen Elizabeth with a free tea for children and old age pensioners. The committee which was set up recommended that a collection should be made and a free tea given to all parishioners, with sports for the children, a bonfire on Woodhills, to be lit by John Clarke of West Chilla (the oldest inhabitant aged 90), and fireworks. Miss Coham–Fleming, who had recently been elected Chairman of the Parish Council (and was to serve in that capacity for 20 years), offered to give each of the school children a commemorative mug. The day started with a peal of the church bells before the 8 o'clock Communion Service. Dr and Mrs. Gwynne arranged for Walter Chapman, the electrician, to put a television set in the School so that all could see the proceedings in London in the morning. The church was full at an united service in the afternoon and the mugs, and medallions donated by Mrs. Jourdan of Beara, were given to the school children before tea, which was followed by sports in Sanctuary field. A social was held in the Public Hall before the bonfire was lit at 11.45 p.m. There was a prize for the best decorated house, which was awarded to Mrs. Knight at Windmilland. In 1911, for the coronation of George V, mugs were given, as well as coronation medals presented by John Risdon, who also gave the church a flag.

A sub-committee was formed in February 1977 to organize the celebration of the Queen's silver jubilee. Ten dozen jubilee mugs were ordered at 45p. each. The day was celebrated on 7th June with a united Church service after which Miss Mabel Beal presented the mugs to children in the school barn. There were sports on the playing field for children in the afternoon followed by tea in the public hall, and in the evening a bonfire on the playing field was lit by Tom Willis, who at 87 was the oldest inhabitant.

To celebrate the conclusion of the second millennium the Parish Council commissioned special mugs at a cost of £5.50. each, which were presented to children of the parish by Mr and Mrs Coham-Fleming at a tea party in the parish hall. This was followed by a firework display in the playing field and a party in the hall with a united service in the flood-lit parish church at 11.30 p.m. Then the church bells rang in the new year – 2000 A.D.

Miss Mabel Beal presenting mugs for the Queen's Jubilee, 1977 with the Parish Clerk, Mrs Ruth Luxton, assisted by Mrs Barbara Lock. Foreground Gary Priest.

THE PUBLIC HALL

In the 1920s several people began to think that a parish hall would be a valuable asset. Hitherto most social events – dances, concerts and public meetings – took place in the schoolroom. No one was more enthusiastic about this idea than the schoolmaster, Mr Leslie Stanbury, to whom fell the greater part of the work of desk-moving and tidying up after events. For many years headmasters had complained about the mess and disorder left after public events were held in the School. In 1914 Mr Fred Eastwick protested to the School Managers that "refuse from a recent dance has been thrown between the school and the doctor's stables which is quite likely to choke the drain running underneath". Mr Stanbury lodged with Miss Mabel Beal at Hillmount, and in 1929 they, together with Marshall Down, George Chapman and others, formed a committee to raise the necessary funds to bring the idea of a public hall to fruition. The earliest minute book dates from February 1930 when Marshall Down was chairman, Leslie Stanbury secretary and James Born treasurer. Mr Down, who was a builder, had drawn plans and the estimated cost was £700, although the eventual bill, including furnishings and fittings, was nearly £1,000.

Many people in the village gave weekly subscriptions and several working men promised their voluntary labour at evenings and weekends. Mr Harry Chapman gave the land on which the old brewery barn stood (opposite The Briary) and the building was soon demolished. On 4th March 1930 tenders were accepted from Marshall Down, Herbert J.Chapman, George Perkins, William Johns and W.C. Harris – builders, carpenters and masons – which amounted to £775. Dances, whist drives and draws were organized. The contractors met on site on 29th March and completion was to be by 15th October. The plan was to build a main hall, a billiard room and ladies cloakroom. The hall would be built onto the old reading room that stood next to Brewery Cottage (the Reading Room was opened sometime in the late 19th century; the earliest reference is in 1893 when Arscott John Isaac is recorded as the secretary).

On 15th May 1930 there was a public luncheon in a marquee seating 150 people in Kelly's Meadow. This was presided over by Mr James Boles, J.P. of

Holsworthy. At 3 p.m. Mrs. Coham-Fleming (the widow of Mr Blyth Coham-Fleming) laid the foundation stone of the Hall. There followed a tea at 5.pm. and then a concert and a dance. The day raised £100. The National Council for Social Service was to be the trustee for the new hall, which was to be named the Black Torrington Public Hall, to be managed by an 18 member committee. The N.C.S.S made available a loan of £250 and the Carnegie Trust made a grant of £130. Eighty bentwood chairs were ordered and wooden benches (both with and without backs). The hall and the billiard room were to be heated by Tortoise stoves, and an electric-lighting plant was supplied by Whitlock's of Holsworthy at a cost of £125. A wash basin and sink were provided and 24 folding card tables were purchased. Walter John Chapman (the second) fixed all the slates in his own time. Likewise Alfie Down, working in the evenings, made all the doors and windows from timber which was supplied.

Strengthening irons had to be inserted between the walls before completion, but the builders kept to their timetable and Opening Day was fixed for 16th October, 1930. The members of the Women's Institute, who were always very supportive of the project and had given a piano for the hall, organized the luncheon and tea, which followed the pattern of the Foundation Day. Mrs. Hynes of Beara Court opened the hall at noon and Mr Scott Browne, from Buckland House, presided at the luncheon. There was a display of folk dancing at 3 p.m. and an auction in the field at 4 o'clock. People gave generously of corn, potatoes, logs and other commodities. There followed a tea and a concert, and a dance at 9pm. The billiard room (later to become the kitchen) was equipped with a billiard table, playing cards, newspapers and books, and became the new men's reading room, under separate control. Pianos did not last very well in the rather damp atmosphere of the hall and replacement instruments were bought or given in 1950, 1959, 1968 and 1983.

The final bill for the Hall was £958.10s. The committee had raised £1,073, but nearly half of this sum was by way of loan; and a year later £442 was still owing to lenders. In December 1930 William Parsons, the baker, was elected chairman. Mr Stanbury was made a life vice president and a life member of the Men's Institute, and was presented with a walking stick in recognition of his contribution. He was soon to leave Black Torrington on his appointment to a new teaching post, and John Adams Isaac became secretary. Charlie Slee was appointed caretaker for £2. 10s. a year with 2s 6d for each meeting! The late Laura Luxton remembered that in the early days, when the lighting was powered by a small engine, there were occasions when Charlie, being tired, switched off the engine and went home. The rooms were soon in total darkness and there was great confusion as people tried to sort out their hats and coats. Fortunately an electricity supply was brought to the village in 1934 and the Hall was connected at the cost of £2.19s.!

Within two months of the Hall opening it was decided that 100 more chairs

Mrs L Coham-Fleming laying the foundation stone fo the Public Hall May 1930. Bill Auberton standing centre left, John Isaac on right.

Mrs C Coham-Fleming laying the stone for the extension in 1980.

were needed. Chairs were not mentioned again until 1959 when the Carnegie Trust made a further grant of £40 to pay for 20 new chairs. In 1931 a skittle alley was added to the amenities, open from 7-10 pm. on evenings when the hall was not booked: contestants paid two pence for 18 balls. It was a rule that women were not to play with men! The Parish Council bought new skittle boards in 1960. In 1931 George Chapman and Samuel Marsh organized a garden show in aid of hall funds. There were sports on Centernhay and a fete in the Rectory garden. In 1933 a urinal and men's lavatory was built on a little piece of land on the east end of the building which was bought from Harry Chapman for £1. In 1934 an entertainment sub-committee of four members was formed which continued to raise extra funds for the Hall for a considerable number of years. One of the early benefits of having a hall was the weekly visit of the travelling cinema, which continued, with occasional breaks, until the 1950s. For some time the films were brought by 'Pettit's Popular Pictures', and during the war, spare parts and new prints, being difficult to obtain, there were frequent break downs and the film sometimes had to be spliced!

John Isaac resigned from being secretary in 1932 and became chairman in 1933. Thereafter the chairmanship rotated every year or alternate year. Miss Mabel Beal became treasurer in 1936, a position that she was to hold for 17 years. In 1937 Herbert Chapman was acting secretary for Mr Bond, the new schoolmaster, who was ill. Mr Chapman continued as secretary for twenty-one years, being paid at first £2 a year for his labour, and from 1947 five guineas. A further loan from the N.C.S.S. of £200 was received in 1937 and in 1938 all those who had loaned money were finally repaid.

About this time the main committee took over the running of the 'reading room'. In 1940 the County Education Authority rented the Hall as an additional classroom for the evacuee children for the sum of £32.10s. per annum. This continued for two years at the end of which time the committee claimed an extra £9 in compensation for damage to the stove. In 1949 mains water supply came to the village and in July the hall was connected to this on the payment of £3. For a number of years from 1943-1958 a children's Christmas party was held in the Hall.

In 1946 there was a proposal to purchase the _old_ reading room (which was being used as a store), and Brewery Cottage and garden from Mr Chapman, but no agreement was reached and the proposal lapsed. The committee continued to rent the old room for storage for £3 a year. Brewery Cottage and garden were finally purchased by the Parish Council for the sum of £25 in 1959. In 1961 a sink unit was added to the 'reading room' which gradually became 'the kitchen'. In that year one third of the annual carnival proceeds were given to the Public Hall and this practice was continued thereafter. In 1963 the old stoves, which had not been functioning well for several years were discarded and a new electric heating system was installed in 1964.

Fancy Dress dance in the 'big' Schoolroom c. 1915
George Copplestone as the huntsman.

Children's Christmas party in the Public Hall c.1955.
Amongst others: Phyllis Ley, Betty Chapman, Pat & Mike Smith, Sylvia Dymond, Freda Harris, Mr & Mrs Stan Baily, Audrey Tucker & Shirley, Margaret Martin, Michael Isaac & Trevor, Mary Chapman & David, Reg Pengelly, Graham Kivell, Alan Jones, Ernest Luxton, Annie Gilbert.

In 1959 Miss Daphne Coham-Fleming was elected chairman and remained in that office for ten years. Thus, for a number of years, she was simultaneously chairman of the Parish Council, Playing Field committee, Carnival committee and Public Hall committee. In 1963, after the trusteeship of the Hall passed to the Parish Council, the Public Hall and Playing Field committees voted to amalgamate but the resolution was never proceeded with. Mr Ralph Hunkin became treasurer of the Hall committee in 1962 and held the position for nearly 40 years. Mrs. Winifred Hatherley was secretary in 1966 and held that office until 1984. In 1967 'Beat' dances were all the rage and resulted in some misbehaviour and rowdyism, so that all such dances held by outside organizations were banned. Hunt Balls however continued to find favour! Also in 1967 the football club was permitted to provide showers for use after games and in 1969 £95 was spent on 60 new chairs. During the 1960s the Women's Institute members organized several Christmas parties for the Senior Citizens. In 1975 some second-hand boards were bought and remodeled into 8 table-tops for which trestles were made; Mr Leslie Allen, who had recently retired to the village did much of this work. In 1978 eighty blue cups, saucers and plates were bought to re-equip the kitchen. In 1980 there was a plan to extend the hall into the car park. A public meeting was called in May and the 87 people present voted in favour of the plans and suggested that the work could be done by voluntary labour. Mr William Ivey offered to saw the timber free of charge and Geoffrey Bowden offered to excavate the ground. Bob Grimshaw and Christopher Lock offered their services and Peter Luxton was asked to undertake the building which he estimated to cost £2,575. A 1p. rate was added to the parish precept which raised £210 and other fund-raising events were held. A bonfire and fireworks display took place on Woodhills on 7th November. On 27th September a second foundation stone, carved by Albert Slade, was laid by Mrs Caroline Coham-Fleming, and Mrs Marshall Down opened the extension on 1st May 1982. The final cost was £3,400.

As the second millennium draws to a close there are suggestions that after seventy years the Hall requires considerable refurbishing and plans are in hand for a new building.

THE PLAYING FIELD

In January 1899 Mr Aubrey Born gave notice that at the next meeting of the Parish Council he would bring forward the question of a Recreation Ground for the children of the village. However, at the meeting in February he withdrew his motion as he was retiring from the Council (which he did in March). The matter was not raised again until 1945 when Mr Winser requested that the Parish Council consider providing a playing field and offered £5, the proceeds of a village social, to start a fund. The Council set up a sub-committee in 1946 with George Copplestone, Herbert and Alfred Chapman and the Parish Clerk.

Sanctuary field was considered the best site, but after unsuccessful attempts to purchase part of the field an approach was made in 1947 to Mrs. Sluggett the owner of Kelly's meadow opposite Long Hall. It was also suggested that part of Mr Coham-Fleming's field to the south might be acquired to allow the provision of a football pitch. By 1949 the ideas were beginning to take their final shape. It was considered that Kelly's meadow would need bulldozing and draining and the dividing hedge would need to be removed and a new boundary made. In 1950 it was agreed to go ahead with these plans using voluntary labour. A purchase price was agreed in 1951 and the Parish Council was to act as trustee for the playing field. The conveyance was made in June 1952 for the sum of £400. Mr Fernley Ivey of Buckpitt made the Parish a loan of £200 to complete the purchase. Mr Coham-Fleming gave the parish part of Venn Meadow. Messrs Brian Down, John Dunford, Leslie Ivey and Don Robinson were nominated to form a fund-raising sub-committee. Brian Down was the chairman and they soon added to their number William Luxton, as treasurer, and Mrs. Dunham, as secretary, and Miss Coham-Fleming. Mr Down was chairman from 1952-58. Miss Coham-Fleming succeeded Mrs. Dunham, as secretary, in 1954, and also assumed the chair after Mr Down relinquished the position.

Messrs Gilbert, Kivell, Perkin and A. Down volunteered to demolish the old shed on the corner opposite Long Hall, to use the stone to fill in the old sewer drain and to make a soakaway. A new entrance gate and flanking walls were

*The cast of The Pageant produced for the opening of the Playing Field, 12th June 1954.
Mr Ernest W Martin, author (extreme right).*

*Miss Coham-Fleming planting the Winston Churchill memorial oak in the Playing Field, 1966.
Watched by the Revd. Sidney Brew, Mr Herbert Chapman, Mr Ernest Broad, Mr & Mrs Morgan,
Mrs Gwynne and children from the School.*

to be built; H. J. Chapman offered to supply the labour. Messrs Gordon Vick were paid £82 for bull-dozing. The surplus money from the Coronation celebration in 1953, amounting to £14.13s., was to be spent on children's swings. Messrs. G. Chapman, B. Down, W. and F. Ivey volunteered to plough, harrow and seed the levelled field. However, more needed to be done. The annual parish meeting in 1953 spent one and a half hours discussing the project. There was still a depression in the centre of the field. A new wall needed to be built against the road on the north side, set back at the corner to improve the visibility. Mr H. J. Chapman's tender of £119.10s. for building a wall and railing on the north side was accepted. A series of whist drives and skittles competitions were held and, in June 1953, a fete at Coham, opened by Mrs Brander-Dunbar, with a whist drive and a dance in the evening made £150 profit. The Coham family gave a wooden seat and the Women's Institute gave another.

At last the playing field was ready for a grand opening ceremony which was set for 2.30.pm on 12th June 1954, and was performed by Miss Daphne Coham-Fleming (Mr Wilfred Pickles, the radio entertainer, was invited but was not able to attend). The opening was followed by a fete with children's sports, and teas in the public hall. At 5 p.m. a Pageant, "Homage to a Community", especially written by Ernest Martin and produced by Mrs. M. Smith and the Revd. Bickford Dickinson, was performed in the field. The costumes were made by members of the Women's Institute. Because the day was dull with intermittent rain the stalls were set up in the garage of The Larches. At 6 p.m. a football match, between Black Torrington and District and Holsworthy and District, was held in Centernhay field. At 8 p.m. there was a whist drive in the Rectory barn and a Grand Dance in the Public Hall with music by the Bideford Arcadian Dance Orchestra and Conjuring by Mr L. Codd of Bradford. A film of the pageant was made in the Rectory barn the next day, and the pageant was repeated on the following Saturday.

In 1955 the Parish Council formed a separate Playing Field Committee comprising the nine councillors. Immediately after the opening the need for equipment for a children's play area was identified and a further surplus from the Coronation Fund, of £38, was made available. Swings and a see-saw were provided, but there were soon complaints that the area was very muddy and it was found necessary to lay an asphalt surface in this area by the entrance gate. A sandpit was added in 1956 and an additional gate for an entrance to the field from the road on the north side was provided. A slide was bought in 1966 and a roundabout and a second cradle swing were added in 1970. There was also a plan to level part of the field for a tennis court, but in 1957 an estimate of £450 for this work was considered too costly. Again in 1973 there were requests for a tennis court, but the estimated cost had risen to £2,000. A football team was started in 1956. Bill Luxton, Colin Kivell and Brian Down all played prominent roles in the formation of the Football Club. Ralph Chapman

Miss Moira Shearer crowning the Carnvial Queen, Thelma Baily, 25th August 1959.
Prince and Princess : John & Mary Baily.
Miss Coham-Fleming standing behind.

was one of the first secretaries, a post later filled by Ruth Luxton. In the first year they paid £5 for the regular use of the pitch, in the second year the charge was rescinded but they were asked to help cut and remove the grass. Grass cutting and drainage proved to be problems from the outset. In 1965 a Forage Harvester was bought and in 1972 a self propelled rotary mower which, at £430, seemed to be a better buy as it was still being used (just) at the end of the century. The field was mole-drained in 1968 and again in 1976. In this year new entrance gates were made by Mr Riches of Hatherleigh at a cost of £84.

In 1967 the Football Club asked permission to erect a shelter on the edge of the pitch behind the cottage gardens of Broad Street: they also wished to play football on Sundays, a request the Committee refused. This question was brought to the Parish Council in 1970. It considered that if play did not coincide with the times of church services there would be no harm. Feeling in the village was obviously not satisfied for the Council took a vote on the question in 1974. There were 5 votes in favour and 1 abstention. However when the Football Club joined the Sunday League in the following year the Committee felt that it should first have asked permission. The Club was also asked to repair and paint the shed, or remove it. The Football Club disbanded in 1980 and was not revived until 1998. In 1974 the Committee issued a set of by-laws for the playing field. These ordered that no cars, dogs or bicycles would be allowed onto the field except by permission, and no activity was to be pursued which was likely to cause damage, and wilful and malicious damage would be an offence.

After the opening of the playing field a cherry tree was planted either side of the entrance; these did not last quite fifty years, an average life span for such a tree. In 1966 the Men of the Trees presented a red oak in memory of Winston Churchill, which was planted by Miss Coham-Fleming and in 1973 they gave a pink chestnut in memory of Group Captain Walker who had given long service on the Devon Association of Parish Councils. In 1971 Mrs. Gwynne gave a maple. These three trees stand along the south eastern boundary of the field and are thriving. Also well-established is a mature horse-chestnut transplanted from her garden by Mrs Joan Trengove in 1986, planted near the car park. In 1989 a small oak was planted on the eastern boundary in memory of "Dorothie" who had spent several happy holidays at Long Hall. On the north west boundary stand a manna ash tree planted in 1990 to replace the old ash tree which had stood at the corner of the field, another horse chestnut and the Millennium Oak which was given by the Parish Council and planted in November 1997.

In 1959 the Parish Council acquired the derelict Brewery Cottage and its garden, which stood between the Public Hall and the Field (see page 118). The Playing Field Committee paid half the cost of purchase, with the Public Hall committee paying the other half. The Council had the cottage demolished and the site levelled for a car park in the early 1960s.

*Henry Bailey (1871-1974) one time stableboy to Parson Jack Russell,
portraying Harvest Home in the Carnival 1959.*

The Fund Raising committee, which was set up in 1952, continued to raise funds for the Playing Field. A Gala Day was organized on 1st October 1955. A Fancy Dress parade took place from the Chapel to the Rectory Barn. There was also skittling on the land beside the Union Hotel, a collection at the football match between Black Torrington and Hatherleigh, a gift auction, tea served in the hall and a social in the evening. This event raised £86.

Emboldened by this success the committee decided to hold a Carnival Week in 1956. The first Carnival Queen, Jean Keast, was crowned on Monday 27th August by County Councillor Mrs. Perkins: this was followed by a six-a-side football match and an entertainment by the Bradford Concert Party. On the Wednesday evening a comic football match was held, followed by a whist drive and a social, held in the Hall and the Rectory Barn respectively. On Saturday there was an Athletic Meeting with side shows, skittles and produce stall with a buffet tea. The Carnival judging followed at 6.30.pm with classes for vehicles, decorated bicycles, walking adults and children. The equestrian class was added in the next year when the carnival procession was led by the Holsworthy Town Band. For a few years both Holsworthy and Northlew Bands attended and for several years the parade included the South Tetcott foxhounds. The carnival continued in a similar form until 1985. The Fundraising committee changed its name to the Entertainments committee and became known as the Carnival committee, with Miss Coham-Fleming as chairman until 1971. In 1959 the film star and dancer, Moira Shearer, crowned the carnival queen, Thelma Baily, and in 1962 the broadcaster and comedian, Jack Train, performed the ceremony. In 1976 a Donkey Derby was held in Centernhay field. The declining number of entries for the carnival led to its abandonment in 1986. The Entertainments/Fund Raising Committee ended its existence in 1998.

There was a confusing overlap between the Parish Council and the Playing Field Committee as the Councillors were also the Committee. This was resolved by the appointment of a Playing Field Management Committee in 1998. In 1996 the Playing Field Committee had decided to build a hard court for tennis if a grant from the Lottery Fund could be obtained. In the process this was expanded to a 'multi-use-games-area' which would be usable for five-a-side football and netball as well. A grant of £27,560 was received from the Sports England Lottery Fund, and the whole project cost £31,200. The new court was opened by John Burnett, M. P. on 17th July 1999.

Sack race at the Jubilee Sports, 1977. Mr Andrew Stacey & Mr Brian Down in the background. The bonfire on the left protected by tarpaulin from the rain!

Northlew Band leads the Carnival procession out of the Playing Field, 1977.

WAR TIMES

Some mention of the First World War has already been made and the erection of a War Memorial. Eight names are inscribed there. As well as George Beal, who died in the battle of the Somme, Melville Chapman, the son of Edgar, was killed in Palestine in 1917 at the age of 25. Four other men born in the village gave their lives: Philip Ward, son of Henry Ward the builder, William Bailey, son of Sanders Bailey the tailor, Fred Perkins, the son of Lewis and younger brother of George, and Walter Isaac the third son of John Isaac. The others commemorated are Harold Ball and Oswald Hopper, who was the grandson of Robert Sanders, veterinary surgeon, of Windmilland.

Robert Freeman Sanders, farrier & horse-doctor, at Windmilland c. 1900.

In 1914 the Parish Council received a request to form a recruiting committee. It felt there was no need as 5% of the population were already serving in His Majesty's forces, but it would encourage further enlistments. In January 1917 a committee was formed to co-operate with the County War Agricultural committee to promote increased production of food, especially growing potatoes and feeding pigs. The committee, under the chairmanship of the Rector, Thomas Buncombe, had some success, for within a week they ordered 2640 lbs. of 'scotch seed' potatoes.

In the Second World War a first aid post was established in the Public Hall, organized by Mrs. Hynes of Beara Court. As early as 1937 an Air Raid Pre-caution Committee had been formed led by the onetime police constable, Albert Winser, who was later Chief Air Raid Warden; it had its post in the lock-up shop opposite Homeleigh in Broad Street. In the winter of 1938 lectures on Air Raid Precautions were given in the Public Hall and in September 1939 all the windows of the hall were, with difficulty, blacked out. In 1942 the Parish Council appealed for Fire Watchers. In the summer of 1939 the Council asked Miss Beal, of Hillmount, if she could make plans to receive 'vacuees' (sic). She asked to be relieved of this responsibility and in 1940 Mrs. Marshall Down and Mr Tom Ivey agreed to help, and in June the evacuees arrived (see Schools). In 1940 the Parish Council organized a collection of old tins and waste paper.

In June 1940, after the defeat of France and the imminent threat of invasion, able-bodied men, mostly farmers and their labourers, formed a company of the Local Defence Volunteers. With their LDV armbands and any shotgun or billhook that came to hand they met to prepare to defend their country from the threat of invasion. By September 1940 they had uniforms and rifles and were named the Home Guard. They were commanded by Major Schofield and Captain Arthur Jones (both from Sheepwash), Sgt. William "Butcher" Isaac and Herbert Chapman. They had an indoor rifle range in the Rectory barn and an open range on the southwest edge of Centernhay field. They manned several roadblocks around the village, had a patrol hut in Hole lane, and an ammunition hut in Woodhills quarry. On most weekends they went out on manoeuvres.

There was only one major incident during the war: a German bomber in 1940, being chased by the R.A.F., dropped a stick of bombs by Gorford and Kingsley. Mrs Broad was injured in the leg by flying shrapnel, a hole was made in the road to Bridge and 6 incendiary bombs threatened a hay store at Smithsland. A non-incident occurred on the night of 3rd July 1940 when the church bells were rung which was the warning signal of an invasion. This turned out to be a false alarm!

The real army came to the village for two months in August 1940. A detachment of the 'Ox & Bucks' regiment (Oxford & Bucks Light Infantry) was billeted in the Rectory barn and stables; and in the glebe field behind, a marquee was erected which served as a mess hall. The military police were stationed in Long Hall barn and there was a searchlight detachment in the field between Beara and Budaire. Coham was also requisitioned by the army for most of the war, the house being used as an officers' mess.

In 1943 the Parish Council was worried lest Dr Gwynne might be called up to serve in the R.A.M.C. which would mean that the nearest doctor would be at Shebbear. The Council wrote a letter to this effect, but in the event call-up never came. During the war years several prisoners, both German and Italian, worked on local farms, some living at the farms and some coming in from the prisoner of war camp at Dobles Lane near Holsworthy.

In 1945 a meeting was called to start a Welcome Home Fund, and in the summer of 1946 Victory celebrations were held in Sanctuary field. In 1947 the Parish Council decided to add to the War Memorial the names of those killed in the 1939-1945 war, to be paid for by public subscription. Albert Slade was commissioned to inscribe five further names: Robert Bridle, who died at Dunkirk, whose mother Elsie married Walter John Chapman after the death of Robert's father, Samuel and Cecil Hooper, who both served in the Royal Navy, Mervyn Hynes, who died in the battle for Syria, and Percy Winser, son of Albert, who was killed in France in March 1945. The work was not completed before 1949 when the Council asked that a sixth name be added, that of Ronald Ham, the son of E.C.Ham (formerly the village baker), who had served in India and Burma.

Centernhay Field c. 1920. Left Henry Beal, second right Mr Henry Mitchell, and right Ernest Chapman. Mr Ernest Chapman lost a leg in the Boer War.

Dancing on The Larches lawn on Club Day c. 1910.

Rifle Club c. 1910.
Front : J Born, T Wheadon, J Moast, Revd. E Donaldson, John Jury, ? , Mr Pope
Middle : Mr Coham-Fleming, Mrs Candler, Mrs Coham-Fleming, ? , Mrs Buncombe,
Sir John Owen, Mrs Coham, Mrs Mitchell, and Mrs Earle.
Back : Dr Candler, Mr Earle, Emily Jury, Mrs Jury, ? , Mrs Chapman, Polly Page,
Mrs Newcombe, ? , Miss A Chapman and the Revd. Thomas Buncombe.

SPORTS AND PASTIMES

The Revd. John Powell, one time Rector of Buckland Filleigh (1875-1920), made copious notes and records; among them is an account of *'outhurling'* in Black Torrington. Hurling still survives as a Shrove Tuesday sport in Cornwall and elsewhere, and involves chasing a ball on foot between certain points in the parish. The local version took place on Whiteleigh meadow after the hay was carried and involved parishioners from Bradford and Cookbury as well as Black Torrington. In the mid-nineteenth century Parson Yule of Bradford had a young Norwegian companion named Randeggar who said there was a similar sport in Norway. The players from the three parishes arranged themselves for the fray that would last several hours. The gentry would ride out on horseback to watch the sport (Mr Powell names Squire George Coham and Parsons John Russell and John Yule). After a few hours some began to fall out, but not the leader. The acknowledged champion of the day was Tom Shadwell (or Stidwell) of Cookbury, a man of "stalwart frame and muscular limbs". After the game all sat down to a much-needed supper at the Bickford Arms at Brandiscorner, frequently joined by the gentry.

About the same time (certainly in the 1880s) there was a racecourse at Kingsmoor and an annual steeplechase was held in July. Later races were held on Coham ham, on the second Thursday in June. Samuel Broad, landlord of the Union Hotel from 1906-1916, would meet the bookmakers at Halwill station in the horse drawn carriage. The day was regarded as a parish holiday with roundabouts, swing-boats and hoop-la, coconut shies, side-shows and sweet stalls in the plot beside the Union Inn. Cricket was also played on the ham in those years and Dr Morgan is said to have organized a club that played there in the 1890s.

Fox hunting may not be considered a sport by all, but it is certainly a pastime. In the Churchwardens' Accounts there are several entries in the 18th century of payments for the killing of foxes. In the reign of Henry VIII a law was introduced to reduce the loss of stock and crops by predators. One shilling was to be paid by the local authority for a fox or badger and lesser

Badminton party in the Rectory Barn, November 1947. Back : Mr Jack Morris (Headmaster Shebbear College), Dr Gwynne, Mr Bickford Dickinson, Revd. B Carver, Revd. Frank Dossetor, Mr Lew Mearns. Front : Mr Bill Moast, Mrs Dickinson, Mrs Morris, Mrs Gwynne, Mrs Fowke, Mrs Dossetor, and Revd. W Fowke.

© Fred Hannaford, Holsworthy

Moving off from the Square after a meet of the South Tetcott Hunt, 28th November, 1959.

Black Torrington AFC 1970

Coffee morning at Beara Court, January 1974.
Among others: Mrs Baxter, Mrs Millman, Mr Percy Dart, Mrs Crossman, Mr Bill Ivey, Mrs Checkley, Miss Daphne Coham-Fleming, Miss Katharine Gwynne, & Mrs Bernice Kivell.

© Braetor Studio

sums for rats, mice, hedgehogs and various birds. In Black Torrington in the 1760s as much as 5/- was paid for a dog fox and 6s.8d. for a vixen. There was organized fox hunting with hounds in the local countryside with hounds being kept by John Arscott of Tetcott as early as the 17th century, but it did not become a very regular sport until the mid 19th ccntury. In 1906 Mr Scott Browne of Buckland Filleigh took over the country which included Black Torrington and built new kennels at Buckland House. For many years the whipper-in for Mr Scott Browne's pack was Ned Chapman of Black Torrington. He was later to become huntsman for the South Devon Foxhounds. In 1916 Mr Browne sold his hounds as he was away on active service. This year saw the formation of the South Tetcott Foxhounds which have hunted this locality ever since.

The earliest sporting club on record is the Miniature Rifle club, founded in 1906 by the Revd. Thomas Buncombe and Dr. George Candler. The first captain was John Jury and the secretary was Thomas Wheadon, the schoolmaster. There was both in-door and outdoor shooting. This continued for some years and the West of England Challenge Shield hung for some time in the Public Hall from the 1930s until competition shooting was resumed after the war, but the Black Torrington club was not revived.

Football became the popular sport between the wars and a local team played regularly until 1953, but did not have a permanent pitch. They played in little Halwill (or Holy Well) field at Long Cross – very muddy – and on the field at Beara now used by the cricket club, and also in the field beside the Torridge by Black Torrington bridge. After the opening of the playing field the club was revived with George Bransom (of the Union Hotel) and Ralph Chapman as secretaries. The club closed in 1980 and shortly afterwards a cricket club was formed and played on the playing field for seven or eight seasons until they transferred their matches to Beara field. The football club was re-started in 1998.

There was a small tennis club started in the 1930s by Herbert Dart who provided a court above Rose Cottage, beyond the churchyard; but the court was not up to competition standard and was later used as a bowling-green. Also before the war badminton was played in the Rectory barn. Capt. Ward Jackson of Kingsley House gave a new (raised) floor for the barn in 1936 to mark the King's Silver Jubilee and steps were built at the old cart entrance. The club was revived after the war but when the school acquired the barn, climbing frames and heaters were fitted and badminton transferred to the Public Hall.

The Girl guides have already been mentioned. After Miss Buncombe left in the 1940s Mrs Joan Dossetor became their leader. When Frank Dossetor returned from serving as an army chaplain, he revived the Scouts troop which had also been started by Miss Buncombe and later led by John Jury, jnr. In the 1990s a company of Brownies, which had met at Beara Court with Mrs Hynes in the 1940s, was reformed. In the 1920s and 30s a branch of the Girls Friendly Society met at the Rectory, with Miss Buncombe, for sewing, knitting and games. A youth club was running in the 1950s and was restarted in 1976 in the Public Hall led by Helen Chapman and Tricia Grimshaw. This has continued intermittently, under various leaders, until the present day.

In 1929 Mrs. Worsley, the doctor's wife, started a branch of the Women's Institute in Black Torrington. In 1989 her daughter, Rachel Worsley, was able to attend its 60th anniversary celebration. The group closed in 1992 and was superceded by a local Women's Group. In February 1977 a group of "over 60s" decided to hold monthly social meetings and called themselves the Jubilee Club (1977 being the Queen's silver jubilee). Mrs. Dorothy Chapman was the Club's first, and only, chairman. It continued meeting until 1988. In 1986 the Church began a social group called 'The Mugs' (a mug of some beverage being offered as refreshment to members by whoever hosted their meetings). In 1988 they presented the first of three variety concerts that they devised to raise funds for local charities, but they did not continue after 1994.

Girl Guides in the 1920s.
Back row second left Gladys Millman, right Janie Dart.

William Down and his son Ben at Long Cross Smithy c. 1900.

DECLINE OF TRADE AND SHOPS

The 20th century brought great changes to trade and business in the country. In 1901 the population of the civil parish was 512. Although there was a slight increase in the next ten years to 586 thereafter the numbers steadily decline until by 1971 the population was down to 380. In the year 2000 it stands at about 480.

The grist (corn) mill at Black Torrington, which for centuries had ground wheat, oats and barley into flour and meal, closed soon after 1912, the last miller being Henry Woodley. Woodhills Brewery, which was established by Mr. Joseph Chapman about 1880, and stood where the Public Hall now stands, only just survived into the 20th Century. The saddlery at Long Hall closed soon afterwards. John Sanders Bailey set up in the village as a tailor and draper about 1880. His father William had also been a tailor in the village in the 1830s. By 1900 he had moved to Malsters Hill as an 'outfitter and clothier' at London house, which later became 'Hillmount'. Another tailor from the 1890s was James Born at the Post Office next to the chapel.

In the mid 19th century a number of brickyards were established in the locality, principally at Petersmarland and at Hatherleigh where the Hunkin family made bricks until 1925. There was a smaller brickyard in Black Torrington at Garlands Moor and another just outside the parish at Winsford. John Dart, a mason from Hatherleigh, settled in Black Torrington about 1870. He was one of those who worked on the construction of Holsworthy viaduct in 1878, walking to work each day from the village. In the 1890s his son Lewis Dart opened a grocery shop at Torridge House. In 1913 he advertised himself as 'grocer, draper, milliner, dealer in butter, eggs and poultry'. The shop continued in the family until Percy and Ruby Dart retired in 1972. The central grocery stores in the village had a much longer life. It was known as 'Hall's shop' in the 1850s. It was then owned by William Horn of Upcott, whose daughter Mary married William Hall. In 1841 the shopkeeper was Joseph Bailey whose daughter Ann had married William Horn. In 1851 the shop was kept by Mary Hall as a grocer and draper, William Hall having 'gone off'. John Braund, the schoolmaster, was at that time her lodger. Mary Hall died in

*Village Stores (RM Snow) with the sun blinds down on the left.
Centernhay Cottage on the right c. 1920.*

*'Lower Darts' shop at Torridge House on the left.
Brookbank Villas on the right 1950s.*

1890 and the shop was acquired by R. M. Snow and Co. of Torrington, who in 1910 advertised 'Grocery, Drapery, Boots, China and General Store'. They kept it until 1925. In the following thirty years there were at least nine different shopkeepers. Those who stayed longest were Percy Phillips (c.1930-45), Freddie Thomas (1959-67), Arthur Perry (1969-78) and Brian Ough (1978-90). It closed in 1993.

Lewis Dart's younger brother, Herbert, learnt his trade as a joiner but went into business in the 20th century fashion, about 1920, becoming a cycle and motor engineer. He already had a small shop at Rose Cottage known as 'Top Dart's' to distinguish it from 'Lower Dart's' at Torridge House. He, and his son John, worked from a shed next to Rose Cottage, below the churchyard. They were also carriers and advertised a hire car. Lewis' son, Percy, ran a small 'bus. Frank Broad (son of Samuel) also ran a garage business, while his brother Ernest, who had driven the carriage and pair for his father, and who became chauffeur to Capt. Ward Jackson, also ran a taxi service. Herbert Dart died in 1930 but his son continued the motor repair business until the second world war. His widow continued the little shop in the front garden of Rose Cottage where she sold ice cream, confectionery and other small items, and this continued until rationing came during the war. In the 1930s John Adams Isaac opened a petrol filling station on the main road at Budaire, and Beara Cross garage was started in 1953 by Stanley Baily.

As wheelwrights became motor engineers so also did blacksmiths become agricultural machinists. The Vanstone brothers, from Buckland Filleigh, established their machine workshop at Devonia in the 1870s. This lasted some fifty years; the work was taken up by Thomas Ivey at Park View, Chilla, after the first world war. The last blacksmith's shop in the village was at Long Cross which closed when Ben Down retired soon after 1950. Agriculture too has changed; with mechanization there are far fewer farm labourers. The remaining farmers (there are effectively only six working farms in 2000) often work in isolation, relying on contractors for many tasks such as harvesting. Several smallholders who formerly kept a few cattle and sheep now let out their grass or have turned to tree planting and other grant-aided schemes. After the first world war George Denford, the village shoemaker, moved from Long Cross to Moor View on the Chilla road. Richard Parsons was another shoemaker in the village until the 1930s. Percy Curtice came from Bradford in 1954 to establish his shoe repair business in the village, and married the district nurse, Miss Rowlands. She had moved into 1, Bowhay on its being built in 1952 and had taken over the duties of nurse Blight who came to the parish after the war as nurse Kilgannon, renting Kingsley Cottage. Percy Curtice had his shop in the front room of the cottage now called Shoemakers until about 1980.

In the 19th century there was a village bun-maker. In the 1880s Elizabeth Badge, a young widow who had earned her living by making gloves, set up a little bakery at Bowhay cottage where she sold yeast buns for two a penny –

Herbert J Dart with a wedding party 1920s.

Cutting corn by hand in a wet year in the 1930s at Windmilland.
Standing : Jim Knight and his nephew Jim
Seated : Walter Luxton, Jack Knight, Mr Daw, 'Grandfather' Jim Knight, Fernley Ball and Mr Glover

one of which was said to be enough for a full meal. It is interesting to note that in 1841 Mary Gilbert is recorded as a baker in 'Bowey' building – perhaps the same cottage? Sometime before 1910 Ernest Ham came to the village from Okehampton and began a more commercial bakery: "Hygenic Steam Bakery" ran the advertisement, "noted for Brown and Currant Bread". He started by delivering from a basket within the village and was soon visiting the neighbourhood with a horse and trap. In 1914 a loaf of bread cost 3¹/₂d. By 1918 the cost had doubled to 7d. however Mr. Ham was able to employ more men and boys and to deliver further afield. He supplied bread, yeast cakes, buns, 'cutrounds' and biscuits. In 1926 he moved to Exeter and sold the bakery to William Parsons who came from Launceston. Mr Parsons expanded the business by making fruit cakes, sponges, pastries and wedding cakes to order. He stayed for some 10 years when he in turn sold the business to Mr Cecil Martin. After the war it became the Black Torrington Bakery, with a manager living at Hamilton House, until it closed in 1961. (Hamilton House had been rebuilt in brick by Marshal Down about 1920).

Besides butchers Isaac and Copplestone there was, in the early part of the century living near the Chapel, Fred Newcombe. He would buy his animals and slaughter them in a shed by the river, delivering the meat to his customers around the district. When Mr Copplestone retired in 1951, Ernest Hatherley came to the Poplars as the village butcher. He continued to have the slaughter house in the sheds opposite until he died in 1965, after which it became part of Walter Chapman's television repair shop (another trade new to Black Torrington in the mid 20th century).

The earliest record of the Post Office is a reference to Mrs Elizabeth Vanstone who was Postmistress at Broom Park cottage in 1841. This was only one year after the introduction of the penny post, pioneered by Rowland Hill, which doubled the volume of postal traffic in one year. Twenty years later Mrs. Vanstone's daughter, Mary who had married Frederick Chapman, was the Postmistress, still at Broom Park cottage. Her daughter, Edith, in turn became sub-post mistress, and married James Born. In 1904 it also became a Telegraph Office and remained in the same place until 1936. It continued there for a little longer with Charles Dart as Postmaster. Then it moved down the road to the cottage now called "Shoemakers", where the Postmaster was Lewis Dart. Later (1952) Mrs. Ham of Briary Cottage took on the Post Office in what had been the Scout hut and ARP room (opposite Homeleigh). When Mr Thomas came in 1959 the Post office was incorporated into the general stores and stayed there until Mr Perry died in 1977. Then it moved again, to Maltsters Cottage, and back to the Stores under Mr Brian Ough and finally to Long Hall in 1994.

The lock-up shop opposite Homeleigh, which had been a Post Office and also a sweet shop has seen many occupants in the last forty years; after some fifteen years as Walter Chapman's television showroom, it has been a butchers, an antique shop, 'DIY' shop, upholsterers and finally a hairdressers.

Above:
Looking down Bonfire Hill to Long Cross Smithy 1910.

Oli & Eli Down at Burrow Farm in 1910

Below:
William Ivey's threshing machine 'Maggie' left in the Rectory Yard. 1956.

Percy Curtice, cobbler outside 'Shoemakers', 1957, with Fred Ball in the background

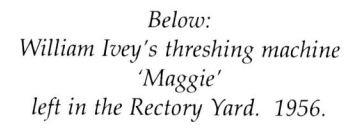

The telephone did not appear to have reached private subscribers until about 1930. In 1935 there were two digit numbers. In 1936 an automatic exchange was opened in Black Torrington which included Sheepwash and part of Highampton. There were twelve Black Torrington subscribers with three digit numbers.

LIST OF SUBSCRIBERS TO THE UNIT AUTOMATIC
EXCHANGE AT BLACK TORRINGTON.
Issued 27/7/36

Rev. T. Buncombe	The Rectory	221
Mr. G. E. Thomas	Coham	223
Mr. L. J. Dart	Torridge House	224
Hole Railway Station	Booking Hall	225
Mrs. F. L. Finnamore	Budaire	226
Capt. C. W. Jackson	Kingsley House	227
Dr. R. G. Gwynne	The Larches	228
Mr. P. F. Phillips	Supply Stores	231
Mr. W. Parsons	Bakery	234
W. Devon & N. Cornwall Farmers Ltd.	Hole Station	238
Mr. A.C. Hynes	Beara Court	241
Police, Devon County	Police Station	244

Before the inception of the Automatic Exchange only the last two digits of the numbers were used. Now, the single property to retain its number, originally 28, is The Larches.

Church Fete : 29th July 1954
Letters of Alphabet Pedlars, amongst whom are, from right to left : Nellie Hunkin (A), Maud Densem (C), Beryl Pedrick (E), Alfreda Chapman (H), Elizabeth Wooldridge (J), Pat Gilbert (K), Betty Thatcher (L), Dorothy Chapman (M), Maureen Bolton (N), Barbara Lake (O), Freda Kivell (P), Susan Johns (Q), Rachel Jury (R), Stella Martin (T), Avril Jones (U), Teresa Stanlake (V), Annie Wivell (W), Kate Osborne (Y). Foreground : Mrs Gwynne, Revd. P Comeau, Mrs Vaux, Dr Gwynne.
Photographed in The Larches Garden

© RL Knight

Sheila Down on her pony in Smithsland farmyard c. 1962

Claude Blight, 1980, rolling hay in Town Meadow, now the site of The Maltings.

INTO THE FUTURE

To end this history of Black Torrington with a chapter on decline may seem a little depressive so I add this envoi. The story is not over: we are in a period of change. The population is again increasing – by the year 2000 the number was about 480, although 40% of these had not lived in the parish for longer than ten years. No longer is there any house without mains electricity, mains water or indoor sanitation; this was not the case when I came to Black Torrington twenty four years ago. The standard of living has risen considerably in the past fifty years: no longer is there any child walking barefoot to school like the little girl from Kingsmoor in the late 1940s. Nearly every family has a refrigerator and a television set whereas in the 1950s only a minority would have these things. The same could be said about the telephone. The number of car owners has also risen dramatically; as late as the 1970s no cars were parked throughout the day and night in Broad Street, although the street itself has now a much better kept appearance.

With the coming of affluence there has been some loss of the community spirit. Until thirty years ago the greater part of the population had been at school with one another locally. Many more services were provided within the village: baker, butcher, cobbler, draper, grocer, ironmonger and garage services were all available. Today there is still a church and two chapels, a public hall and a good playing field, one garage, a part time post office and shop, a public house, a school and a surgery, but some of these are under threat.

In 1987 District Councils began to make 'Local Development Plans'. The plan published in 1988 showed land designated for housing development in addition to the Harry's Meadow site which already had planning permission for 9 dwellings. Fields to the south of both Harry's Meadow and the Playing Field, and another behind the chapel, were designated. A field at Long Cross was identified specifically for 'employment development'. There was an uneasy feeling among many in the parish that this might lead to over-development and as a result, in November 1988 a Residents' Association was formed with Dr Filer Cooper as chairman. The Revd. Gerry Matthews succeeded him as chairman in the following year. The Association together with many individuals made objections to the plan when it was published in 1989 and there was a Public Inquiry in March 1990 after which all the land with the exception of a piece of the field to the south of Harry's Meadow, was withdrawn. The Association continued for a few years, published an information leaflet about all the facilities and societies that served the parish, helped to organize the hospital car service and encouraged efforts for the 'best kept village' competition. But with its main aim accomplished it went into abeyance after eight or nine years. Perhaps it might be revived?

We have a rich heritage: it is for the people of Black Torrington to join together to preserve and enhance what we already have. For those who appreciate country life it is a quiet and pleasant place in which to live and I commend it to the future – for another thousand years.

Black Torrington 2000 AD

APPENDICES

1. Rectors and Patrons of the Parish of Black Torrington.

Date of appointment	Rector	Reason for vacating the benefice	Patron
1277/8	Henry Fitzwarren		Sir Roger la Zouche, kt.
c.1295	William de Flore		
1308	Robert Pollard		
1313/4	Elias de Tyngwyke		Sir Alan la Zouche, kt.
1315	Walter de Cromhale		Sir Nicholas de St Maur, kt.
1331	William, a monk		
1344	John de Wike		Sir Alan de Cherletone, kt.
1355	Griffin de Cherletone	resigned	Sir Alan de Cherletone, kt.
1357	Thomas de Byschebury		Sir Alan de Cherletone, kt.
1359	William Poltone		Sir Alan de Cherletone, kt.
1361	William Falewille		K.Edward III (for the heir of Nicholas Seymor)
1370	Thomas de Sekyndone	exchanged	K.Edward III (for the heir of Nicholas Seymor)
1380/1	Simon de Morecote	died	Sir Richard Seymour, kt.
1390/1	John Wyndoute, a monk	exchanged	Sir Richard Seymour, kt.
1404/5	David Lovering		Lady Ela de St Maur
1430	Robert Wyot	resigned	King Henry VI
1430/1	William Estby	died	King Henry VI
1437	John Coke (alias White)		John de St Maur
?	Thomas Faulkner	resigned	
1459	John Webber	resigned	Sir Thomas St Maur, kt.
1498	Robert Nokeworthy (possibly)		
?	John Mugworthy	died	
1514	John Yowe (or Yeo)	died	Willm. Preston de Burdeport
1543	Thomas Yonge	died	John Bushope
1569/70	Richard Bampfelde		Richard Bampfelde
1585	George Closse, M.A.	degraded	Queen Elizabeth I (by lapse)
1615	Richard Bowden	died	Amyas Bampfield
1626	Thomas Clifford, B.D.	resigned	The Bishop
1627/8	James Bampfylde, M.A.	died	
1663	James Lake, B.A.	died	Sir Coplestone Bampfylde, bart.

1. Rectors and Patrons of the Parish of Black Torrington (continued).

Date of appoint-ment	Rector	Reason for vacating the benefice	Patron
1712/3	John Bradford, M.A.	died	Sir C. Warwick Bampfylde, bart.
1737	John Carew, M.A.	resigned	Sir Richard W. Bampfylde, bart.
1762	John Burgess, B.A.	died	Sir Richard W. Bampfylde, bart.
1781	Denys Yonge	resigned	Sir Charles W. Bamfylde, bart.
1783	Richard Warwick Bampfylde, M.A.	died	Sir Charles W. Bamfylde, bart.
1834	John Penleaze, B.A.	died	John Story Penleaze
1879	John Russell, B.A.	died	Lord Augustus Poltimore
1883	John Samuel Jephson Gardiner, M.A.	died	Robert Holmes Jephson
1907	Thomas Buncombe, M.A.	died	Mrs Clara Gardiner
1941	Roberts Francis Dossetor, B.A.	resigned	Dr Arthur Gardiner
1949	Percival Comeau, A.K.C.	resigned	Diocesan Board of Patronage
1959	Courtenay Johns	resigned	Diocesan Board of Patronage
1964	Robert Sidney Brew, B.Sc.	(Priest-in-Charge)	
1973	Ronald Harry Baker	resigned	Diocesan Board of Patronage
1978	Gerald Lancelot Matthews	(Priest-in Charge)	
1991	Howard John Mayell	(Priest-in Charge)	
1997-	David Michael Wood	(Priest-in Charge)	

2. 1332 Lay Subsidy – Black Torrington list.

(Voted by Parliament for Edward III to fight the war in France)

Taxed @ 2s.	Thomas de Waunford Martin Broun Elias Glovyle	Taxed @ 10d	Walter de Couham Thomas de Cromhale Robert atte Crosse Richard Chill
Taxed @ 16d	Henry de Midelkote		Michael Bokkeberd Henry de Graddon
Taxed @ 1s.	Almeric fitz Waryn Henry atte Heghen William Penne Hugh atte Forde John atte Coue		John Frenche John Gellan Adam atte Forde John Whita
	Robert de Middelcote John Sutore Henry Beaumond William le Zouche	Taxed @ 8d.	Adam de Bokeputte John le Zouche John de Kynalonde William atte Trewe

3. 1569 Devon Muster Roll.

Presenters for Black Torrington: Thomas Parson, John Haysed, Lewis Burden, Christopher Elbury.

Assessed to provide arms on income from land between £10-£20: Thomas Parson & John Haysed.

Assessed to provide arms on income from goods (£10-£20): Lewis Burden, Robert & Richard Brawne, John Kinge, Thomas & Richard Olyver and Nicholas Stenlake.

Archers:	Richard Yorland, gent.	Harquebusiers:	John Beareman
	Stephen Burden		Robert Olyver
	William Cockerham, jnr.		John Arnell
	Simon Horwill		Gilbert Smale
	John Stenlake, jnr.		Robert Walter
	Stephen Stenlake		Richard Ellice
	Lawrence Stenlake		Lawrence Nosewethye
	John Norlighe		George Tawton
	John Hayne		John Hooper, jnr.
	Edmund Collacotte		Richard Hooper
			William Dynsham
Pikemen:	William Vowdon	Billmen:	Richard Oliver
	Henry Haysed		John Tayller
	Christopher Dynsham		John Tawton
	John Dynsham		

4. 1641 Signatures to the Protestation.

John Courtier	minister.
Humphrey Smale	churchwarden.
Stephen Coham	
William Battin	constables.
William Cockram,	
Robert Hesed	
George Smale	overseers.

and:

Faithful Averye	Gregory Frye	Robert Oliver, snr.
Nicholas Axworthye	John Frye	Robert Oliver, jnr.
William Badge	Leonard Frye	Thomas Oliver
Clement Ball	Lewis Frye	Edmund Paige
Tristam Basset	Lewis Fylberte	John Paige
Lewis Battyn	Abraham Gilberte	Richard Paige, snr.
John Beale	John Gilberte	Richard Paige, jnr.
John Bickle, snr.	Lewis Gilberte	Thomas Paige
John Bickle, E.Chille	John Glasse	John Palmer
John Bickle, jnr.	Thomas Glawen	William Parishe

4. 1641 Signatures to the Protestation (continued).

John Robert Bickle Esq.
Robert Bickle, jnr.
Roger Bickle
Thomas Bickle
William Bickle
Richard Blighte
John Brand, snr.
Hugh Brande
John Brande
Thomas Brande
John Brooke, snr.
John Brooke, jnr.
George Browne
Robert Browne
Shadrach Browne
William Browne, snr.
William Browne, jnr.
Humphrey Burdon
John Burdon, snr.
John Burdon, jnr.
Leonard Burdon
Lewis Burdon
William Burdon
William Button
Humphrey Calwell
William Chugge
John Cloake
Arthur Collins
Jeremy Colwell
Robert Colwell
Samuel Davye
Robert Dawe
William Densam
Abel Downe
Nathaniel Downe
Ambrose Drewe
Robert Dunne
Christopher Elburye
John Elburye
Robert Elburye
Abraham Frye

John Gorforde
John Gusham
Thomas Gusham
Henry Hatherly
Lewis Hatherlye
Thomas Hayne
John Heane
Lewis Hele
Thomas Hele
William Hele
John Hesed, snr.
John Hesed, jnr.
Philip Hooper
Richard Hopkins, snr.
Rice Hopkins, jnr.
John Hopper
Oliver Hopper
John Hutchins
Richard Jeffrye
James Jenkin
Evans Johns
Christopher Kinge
Humphrey Kinge Esq.
Humphrey Kinge, jnr.
John Kinge
William Kingwell
Emmanuel Lavackedaye
Humphrey Loveis, gent.
William Luxmore
Lawrence Madge
John Maye
William Maye
Michael Mitchell
Roger Morris
Richard Mounsell
William Norlye
Richard Norlye
George Oliver
John Oliver, East Chill
John Oliver, jnr.
Robert Oliver, East Hill

John Parsons, jnr.
Thomas Parsons
William Parsons
George Pine
Edmund Poslet
John Poslette
Samuel Quicke
Alexander Rewe
Stephen Rewe
John Risdon
Lewis Risdon
Robert Risdon
Nicholas Rolston
Robert Rowcliffe, snr.
Robert Rowcliffe, jnr.
William Segar
Fulke Smale
George Smale
John Smale
John Smale, jnr.
Robert Smale, snr.
Robert Smale, jnr.
Robert Smale of Leigh
Thomas Smale
William Smale
George Soper
Peter Soper
Richard Soper
Robert Squire
William Stenlake
John Stronge
John Tanton
Joseph Tanton, snr.
Joseph Tanton, jnr.
Richard Thomson
George Tillye
Simon Tillye
Edward Waterman
Richard Waterman
Samuel Webber
Rowland Williams

5. Churchwardens of Black Torrington Parish Church.

(In most of the early years only the name of one churchwarden is recorded)

1612	Lewis Coham	1805	John Ward & Hugh Balkwill	1850-1	George S. Risdon & John Yelland
1641	Humphrey Smale	1806	Richard Paige & Richard Balsdon	1852-9	George S. Risdon & John Tanton
1726	James Short	1807	James Tanton & John Baily	1860-1	John Tanton & Amos Parsons
1737	Richard Standon	1808	James Johns & George Paige	1862	John Tanton & George S. Risdon
1738-9	Richard Olliver of East Chilla	1809	James Paige & Edward Morcombe	1863-8	George S. Risdon & George Braund
1740-1	George Olliver	1810	Anthony Tucker & Lewis Horn	1869-71	George S. Risdon & James Sparke
1742	Peter Standon	1811	George Piper & Lewis B. Horn	1872-3	George S. Risdon & Bickford Coham Esq.
1743-46	Richard Olliver	1812	John D. Burdon & Elias Leach, snr.	1874-82	George S. Risdon & James Sparke
1747-8	George Smale	1813	Martyn Chapman & Hugh Balkwill	1883-6	Joseph Chapman & James Sparke
1749	Jonas Parsons	1814	John Marsh & Amos Parsons	1887-95	Edwin Risdon & James Sparke
1750-1	John Burdon	1815	Samuel Bassett & Thomas Hobbs	1896-1908	Lucius H. Reichal & Joseph Chapman
1752	John Heysett	1816-17	Charles Knight, jnr. & Lewis Ward	1809-13	James Risdon & Joseph Chapman
1753-4	Isaac Johns	1818-19	Arscott Braund & Edward Morcombe	1914-21	James Risdon & Henry Beal
1755-6	Humphry Braund	1820	Richard Balsdon & John Chapman	1922-4	Alfred Kelly & Henry Beal
1757-8	James Short	1821	Hugh Balkwill & George Smale Risdon	1924-7	George Copplestone & Henry Beal
1759-61	Peter Paige	1822	Anthony Tucker & George Paige	1928-9	George Copplestone & John Jury
1762	Jonas Parson	1823	Edward Morcombe & Richard Balsdon	1929-36	George Copplestone & James B. Born
1763-5	George Smale	1824-5	Hugh Balkwill & George S. Risdon	1936-56	George Copplestone & John Jury
1766-7	Anthony Cornish	1826-31	Hugh Balkwill & Arscott Braund	1957-66	John Jury & Anthony Thatcher
1768-70	Robert Heysett	1832-4	Arscott Braund & George Paige	1967-71	Anthony Thatcher & Colin Kivell
1771-4	Humphry Braund	1835	Arscott Braund & Anthony C. Tucker	1972	Colin Kivell & Leslie Ivey
1775-7	Elias Leach	1836	Robert Leach & James Tanton	1973-9	Colin Kivell & Clifford Baily
1778-80	Anthony Cornish	1837	George S. Risdon & George Paige	1980-1	William. Coham-Fleming & Clifford Baily
1781-6	John Stenlake	1838	William Chapman	1982-91	William. Coham-Fleming & Leslie Allen
1787	Joseph Chapman	1839-43	John G. Maxwell & George S. Risdon	1992	Peter Mayer & Leslie Allen
1788	Anthony Cornish	1844	John G. Maxwell	1993-5	Peter Mayer & Katharine Matthews
1789	Alexander Martyn	1845	George S. Risdon & George Braund	1996-2000	Christopher Lock & Katharine Matthews
1790	Elias Leach & Lewis Horn	1846-7	John G. Maxwell & George S. Risdon		
1791	John Denis Burdon & James Balsdon	1848-9	George S. Risdon & Samuel Hunkin		
1792	James Hearn & James Risdon				
1793	Hugh Balkwill & John Stanlake				
1794	John Pidler & John Ward				
1795	Richard Paige & Richard Balsdon				
1796	Samuel Johns & Thomas Bayley				
1797-9	John Denis Burdon & Joseph Chapman				
1800	Elias Leach, snr. & Lewis Ward				
1801	Anthony Tucker & Lewis Horn				
1802	John Marsh & Amos Parsons				
1803	George Braund & James Hearn				
1804	Elias Leach & Hugh Balkwill				

6. Head Teachers of Black Torrington School.

John Braund	circa 1840 – 1872
George Passmore	1875 – 1876
Garth Chapple	1877 – 1881
Samuel Penwarden	1882 – 1890
Robert E. Mills	1890 – 1902
E. J. Foxcroft	1903 – 1904
Thomas R. Wheadon	1904 – 1911
F. Thornton Eastwick	1912 – 1917
John W. Heard	1920 – 1925
Leslie J. Stanbury	1925 – 1930
N.F.A. Bond	1931 – 1937
Thomas Glasson	1937 – 1951
(absent on war service with the R.A.F.	1940 – 1946)
Mr George Eades (acting head)	1942 – 1945
Miss S. Chapman	1953 – 1954
Mrs Joan Robinson	1955 – 1956
Raymond C. Kayes	1957 – 1961
David F. Deans	1961 – 1965
Bruce M. G. Hall	1965 – 1969
James Rourke	1970 – 1983
Neville Gelling	1983 – 1992
Peter Forrest	1992 – 1995
Mark Raven	1995 –

(This list does not include temporary and acting heads except Mr Eades)

7. Doctors (having a regular surgery in Black Torrington)

Arthur Willoughby Owen, M.R.C.S.L., L.A., H.L.	circa 1850-1885
Henry Heath Parsloe, M.R.C.S.(Eng), L.R.C.P.(Edin)	1886-1887
Arthur Lucas Morgan, M.R.C.S.(Eng), L.R.C.P.(Edin)	1887-1893
Edward Macready Spencer, L.R.C.P., L.R.C.S.(Edin), L.F.P.S.	1893-1895
Julian Henry White, L.S.A.(Lond)	1896-1899
Francis Whitelaw, M.R.C.S.(Eng), L.R.C.P.(Lond)	1899-1903
George Candler, M.R.C.S., L.R.C.P.(Lond), L.S.A.	1903-1928
Reginald Carmichael Worsley, M.R.C.S.(Eng), L.R.C.P.(Lond)	1929-1931
William Michael, M.B.,B.Ch.	1931-1933
Richard Gordon Gwynne, M.R.C.S.(Eng), L.R.C.P.(Lond)	1933-1971
Roger Filer Cooper, M.B.,B.S., L.R.C.P., M.R.C.S.	1971-1990
Asad Al-Doori, M.B.,Ch.B., M.R.C.G.P.	1990-

8. War Memorial.

There are 14 names on the Black Torrington War Memorial:

1914-1918
George Cutland Beal, son of Henry Beal, died in the Somme 18th October 1916,
aged 32 years. Gunner, 4th Worcestershire Regiment.
William Charles Bailey, son of Sanders Bailey, died 27th October 1916,
aged 29 years. Sapper, Royal Engineers.
Frederick Harold Perkins, son of Lewis Perkins, died l6th October 1917 in Belgium,
aged 28 years. Shoeing Smith Corporal, Royal Field Artillery.
Melville James Chapman, son of Edgar Chapman, died 3rd December l917 in
Palestine, aged 25 years. Private, Devonshire Regiment.
Walter James Isaac, son of John Isaac, died 2nd April 1918 in France,
aged 22 years. Private, Duke of Cornwall's Light Infantry.
Oswald R.L. Hopper, son of John Hopper, died 27th May 1918 in France,
aged 18 years. Private, Royal Berkshire Regiment.
Philip Ward, son of Henry Ward, died 2nd October 1918 in France,
aged 42 years. Sapper, Royal Engineers.
Harold S. Ball,

1939-1945
Robert C. Bridle, son of Charles Bridle, died on the beach at Dunkirk, May 1940.
Grenadier Guards.
Mervyn Arthur Hynes, son of Arthur Cecil Hynes, died 11th July 1941 in Syria,
aged 27 years. 2nd Lieut. North Somerset Yeomanry.
Samuel John Hooper, son of Samuel Hooper, died 27th February 1942,
aged 21 years. Leading Stoker, R.N. (H.M.S. *Jupiter*)
Ronald Grey Ham, son of Ernest Ham, died 31st May 1944 in India,
aged 29 years. Private, Somerset Light Infantry.
Cecil Wallace Hooper, son of Samuel Hooper, died 6th September 1944,
aged 22 years. Able Seaman, R.N. (H.M.S. *Batavia*)
Percy Owen Winser, son of Albert Winser, died 12th March 1945 in France,
aged 26 years. Private, Pioneer Corps.

George William Cliffe, Seaman, R.N.R. died August 1942,
aged 25 years, is named on the memorial in the parish church.

9. Chairmen of the Parish Council.

1894-1919	Henry Beal	farmer	Bridge
1919-28	William Spear Isaac	butcher	The Poplars
1928-9	John Jury	carpenter	Long Cross
1929-36	James Bawden Born	tailor	Broompark Cottage
1936-46	George Copplestone	butcher	The Poplars
1946	Edgar Anthony	farmer	Fraunch
1946-9	William Slade	farmer	Hole Farm
1949-50	James Knight	farmer	Windmilland
1950-52	Herbert Chapman	builder	Kneela
1952-3	George Chapman	farmer	Upcott
1953-73	Daphne Coham-Fleming		Coham
1973-84	Roger Filer Cooper	doctor	Coham Bridge
1984-89	Charles Ley	farmer	Hope Farm
1989-94	Peter Ellis	agricultural merchant	Wistaria
1994-95	Christopher Tweedale	teacher	Broompark
1995-96	Gerald Matthews	priest	The Larches
1996-97	Jeremy Ions	surveyor	Rose Cottage
1997 –	Gerald Matthews	priest	The Larches

10. Carnival Queens.

1956	Jean Keast		1970	Maureen Tucker
1957	Lorna Jones		1972	Sheila Willis
1958	Jane Clare		1973	Deborah Garisch
1959	Thelma Baily		1974	Beverly Barber
1960	Kathleen Metters		1975	Susan Jones
1961	Anne Johns		1976	Julia Hannaford
1962	Heather Kivell		1977	Susan Baily
1963	Elizabeth Knight		1978	Deidre Blair
1964	Nora Chapman		1979	Kathryn Ellis
1965	Eileen Daniel		1980	Mandy Colwill
1966	Velma Millman		1981	Jean Wonnacott
1967	Sheila Down		1982	Rosalind Smith
1968	Shirley Tucker		1983	Nicola Grimshaw (Princess)
1969	Diane Chapman		1984	Angela Luxton

INDEX

A
Abbott, Miss 98
Acland, Thomas 58
Adams, Edwin and John 75
Addlehole 44
Adkins, Ronald 93
Al-Doori, Asad 63
Allen, James 42, Leslie 120
Allin, John 41, 45, William 45
Alwold 14
Andrew, Emily 91, Philip 47, Samuel 81
Arscott, John 38, 136
Arundell, William 53
Ashburton, Lord 47, 53
Ashbury 13, 49
Ashton, Elizabeth 57
Ashwater 73, 91, 97, 106
Avery, John 78, 88, 95

B
Back Lane 41, 97-8, 104, 108, 110
Badge, Elizabeth 75, 141, John and Mary 75
Bailey, Ann 139, Henry 61, 126, John 103, 106, 139, Joseph 45, 97, 139, Sanders 129, William 129, 139,
Baily, Claud, Pam, Reg & Ron 69, Clifford, 110, Jeanette 92, John & Mary 124, Richard 54, 107, Stanley 110, 119, 141, Thelma 124, 127,
Baker, Ronald 93-4,
Baldwin, de Brion 15
Balkwill, Ann 57, Florrie 100, Hugh 41, 82,Stephen 93
Ball, Fernley 142, Fred 76, 144, Harold 129
Balsdon, David 103, John 42, Richard 24, 47, 53, 79, 102, Susan 47, William 18
Bampfylde, Amias 33, Benoni 38, 95, Charles 44, 81, Coplestone 38, Edward 37, Elizabeth 34, 37, George 81, James 34-35, 37, Mary 33, 37, Richard 28-29, 31, 38, 44, 49, 79-81, William 23,33,
Bampfylde House 33
Baptists 97-98, 103
Barkwill, Pam & Reg 70
Bastard, Edmund 58
Bate, Michael 77
Batson, Rupert 11
Battin, William 35
Bawden, Gertrude 104
Beal, George 91, 129, Henry 91, 103, 107, 131 Mabel 102,113-115, 118, 130
Beara 18, 29, 32-33, 35, 40, 49, 66, 86, 113, 116, 130-131, 135 136,145
Beara Cross Garage 141
Beare, Jack and John 60
Beaworthy 13
Bible Christians 97-99
Bickersteth, Bishop 88
Bickford, Arscott and Mary 47
Bickle, John and Robert 35
Bishoppe, John 34
Blackley 47,101-102
Blake House 63
Blight, Bessie 96, Claude 77, 146, George 54, Mary 63, Nurse 141
Boles, James 115
Bond, Henry and Thomas 42, N.F. 118
Bonfire Hill 97, 99, 103-104, 106, 113, 144
Born, Aubrey 88, 103-104, 121, Frederick 90, James 104, 106-107, 115, 132, 139, 143, Nellie 69, Richard 49, 104, Robert 104
Bovacott 38, 44, 49
Bowden, Geoffrey 120, Richard 33-34
Bowhay 63, 112, 141
Bowhay Cottage 141
Bradford 13, 15-16, 38, 42, 45, 51, 62, 93, 98-99, 103, 127, 133
Bradford, John 38
Brander-Dunbar, Mrs 123
Bransom, George 136
Bratton Clovelly 59
Braund, Arscott 47, George 45, 51, Hockin 47, 51, Joan 30, John 30, 41, 65, 139, Lewis 30, 51, Richard 29-30, Thomas 47, Robert 29, 31, William 21, 30

Braundsworthy 18, 30, 33, 39, 47, 51
Brent, William 45
Brew, Sidney 122
Brewery 56, 139
Brewery Cottage 70, 115, 118, 125
Briary Cottage 41, 57, 65, 113, 115, 143
Brickyards 139
Bridge Farm 31, 33, 36, 47, 49, 91, 103, 130
Bridle, Elsie and Robert 131
Bright, Eliza 74
Broad, Dorothy 130, Ernest 92, 122, 141, Frank 141, Samuel 54, 60, 133
Broad Street 20, 22, 33-34, 41, 49, 63, 66, 108, 110, 112, 125, 130, 147
Broadhurst, F 60
Brock, Richard 59
Broompark 98
Broom Park Cottage 104, 143
Bryant, Roger and Vera 63
Buck, George and Lewis 49
Buckland Filleigh 9, 38, 47, 51, 53, 86, 101, 136, 141
Buckpitt 18, 33, 43, 47, 49, 97, 103-104, 107, 121
Buckpitt, Mary 57
Budaire 131, 141, 145
Buddle Lane 104
Buncombe, Annie 93, 132, Helen 93, 136-137, Thomas 91, 93, 130, 132, 136, 145
Burdon, Charles 18, 25, 41, 49, Edmund 27, Elizabeth 30, 38, John 29, 30, 41, John Denis 28, 49, 79, Leonard 29, Lewis 29, 31, 35, Nicholas 27, Robert 29, 41, Stephen 29
Burgess, John 42-44, William 42
Burnett, John 127
Burrough 32
Butler, A. 11
Butterbear 18-19, 33, 47, 54, 104, 107

C
Calloway & Co 98
Candler, Edith 61, 132 George 61-62, 75, 132, 136
Carew, John 38, 42
Centernhay 32, 59, 103, 112, 118, 123, 127, 130-131
Centernhay Cottage 104, 140
Chapell, Laura 66
Chapman, Alfred 98, 113, 121, Betty 70, 119, Cecil, Gwen, Ivy & Sidney 69, Dorothy 92, 137, 145, Edgar 98, 129, Edith 104, 143, Edmund 98, 136, Ernest 55, 107, 131, Frances 72, Frederick 65-66, 103, 143, George 72, 107, 109, 115, 118, 123 Harry 108, 113, 115, 118, Helen 137, Herbert 55, 110, 115, 118, 121-123, 122, 130 John 98, Joseph 24, 42, 47, 51, 53-55, 79-80, 97, 105, 112,139 Margaret 64, Mary 104, 119, Melville 129, Nora 92,102 Ralph 10, 70, 123, Stephen 92, 109 136, Walter 88, 113, 116, 131, 143, William 24, 47, 54, 61, 99
Chapple, Emily and Garth 65
Chestnuts, Chilla, 66
Chilcott, Harry 76
Chilla 15, 18, 33, 35, 44-45, 47, 49, 54, 66, 75, 98-99, 103, 106, 112 113, 141
Chilla Chapel 66, 75
Chilla House 98
Chilla School 72, 96, 104
Chudleigh, James 36
Church Lands 41-42, 57, 101
Claremont 57
Clarke, David 53-54, 99, John 113, Miss 91, William 99, 103
Clemetts, William 45
Cleverdon, Leslie 69
Clifford, Thomas 34
Clinton, Lord 79
Closse, George 22, 31-32
Cockram, William 35
Codd, Leslie 123
Coham 17, 27, 33, 38, 40, 44, 49, 57, 60, 76, 123, 131, 145
Coham, Arscott 82, Arthur 38, Augusta 82, George 44, 46, 51, 58, 133, Holland 38, 42, 44, 49, 81, John 27, 38, 41 Lewis 32,34, 38, 42, Margaret 38, Mary 82, Stephen 27, 32 35, 38, 41, 80, 82, Susanna 38, Thomas 27, 30, 34, Walter 19, William 42, William Bickford 26, 51, 54, 58, 80-82, William Holland 44, 47, 49, 51, 54, 79-80, 97, 105, W.H. Bickford 44, 51, 54, 65

Coham-Fleming, Bickford 107-108, Blyth 54, 91, 102-103, 132, Caroline 117, 120, Daphne 110, 113, 120-125, 127, 135 Elinor 54, Lilian 116-117, William 11, 55, 113, 121
Coham Bridge House 63
Comeau, Maurice 93, Percival 93, 145
Commercial Hotel 53, 58-59
Cooper, Groves 53
Copplestone, George 55, 93, 106, 112, 114, 119, 121, 143, Teresa 69
Coram House 104
Courtier, John 34-35
Crabhay 108
Craythorne 18
Creper, Harriet 61
Cripple (Cromhale) 18, 45
Cromhale, Walter de 22
Curtice, Percy 141, 144

D
Damrell, James 97
Dart, Charles 143, Courtenay, 70, Edie 91-92, 102, Herbert 136, 141-143, Jacqueline 70, Jane, 137 John 45, 139, Lewis 105, 107, 139, 141, Percy 135, 139, 141
Davidson, John 80
Davils (Davylles) 17-19, 29, 31, 53
Daw, John 48-49, 66, 101
Dawe, James 45
Denford, George 45, 66, 141
Devon Militia 79
Devonia 76, 103, 141
Dickinson, Bickford 81, 123, 134
Donaldson, Edward 88, 91, 132
Dossetor, Frank 93, 134, 136, Joan 134, 136
Down, Ada 96, Albert 99, Alfred 116, 121, Ben 138, 141, Brian 10, 110, 121, 123, 128, Elsie 102, 120, 130, Henry 45, James 45, 99, John and Robert 47, Marcia 69, Marshall 72, 107, 115, 143, Maurice 70, Oli 111, 144, Sheila 146, Thomas 99, William 138
Drake, William 95
Ducking (or Cucking) stool 61, 104, 110
Dufty, Miss 98
Dunford, John 110, 121
Dunham, Mrs 121
Dunsland 15, 47, 49, 80-81
Durrant, Christopher 41
Dymond, Sylvia 70, 119

E
East Lake 44, 49
East Street 108, 110
Eastern Hamlet 49, 103
Eastwick, Thornton 72, 115
Ebrington, Lord 58
Edmar 15
Elburie, Christopher 29, 31
Evacuees 72, 130, 118

F
Facey, Alex 97
Filer Cooper, Roger 63, 110, 147
Fisher, Thomas 53, 65
Fishleigh 31, 33, 104
Fitzwarren, 17-19
Fleming, John 54
Football Club 123, 125, 135
Forda 18, 33, 47, 54, 65, 107
Fortescue, Lord 82
Fourth of June Club 59
Fox's Orchard 97, 104
Fraunch 47, 75-76
Frazer, Madelaine 91
Frye, Abraham 34
Fulford, Medley 88
Furse, Richard 57

G
Gardenia 113
Gardiner, Arthur 93, Clara 86-87, 91, Jephson 66, 86-88, 90-91, 102
Garlands Moor 139

Gay, John 47
Gilbert, Annie 119, James 47, 49, 57, 81, Mary 47, 65, 141, Noah 121, Pat 145, Philip and Richard 57
Gillett & Bland 82
Gillett & Johnstone 93
Glasson, Thomas 70, 72-73
Glubb, Blanch 38
Gorford 33, 103-104, 110, 130
Gortleigh 53
Graddon 18, 31, 33, 43, 47, 49, 75
Grimshaw, Bob 120, Tricia 137
Gullett, John 18
Gwynne, Richard 62, 77, 113, 131, 134, 145, Muriel 70, 122, 125, 134, 145, Katharine 135

H
Hall, Bruce 73, Mary 139, William 47, 139
Halwill 13, 42-44, 49, 54, 77, 81, 99, 106-108, 133
Ham, Bernard 92, Edith 143, Ernest 112, 141, 143, Harry 92, Henry 39, Ronald 131
Hamilton House 105, 143
Harold, earl 14
Harris, Abraham 45, Arthur 19, Freda 119, John 35 Samuel 43, 77, Thomas 43, William 53, 80, 115
Harry's Meadow 112, 147
Hartland Abbey 49
Hatherleigh 18, 21, 36, 45, 58, 65, 73, 81, 97-98, 125, 127, 139
Hatherly (Hatherleigh) Ernest 143, George 43, John and Philip 41, Winifred 120
Hawkey, Richard 99
Hayne 18, 33, 47, 101, 106
Hayne (Haine) Catherine 27, 31, Thomas 27
Heanton Satchville 79
Heard, John 72, Nathaniel 55, Richard 45
Hearn, Anne 95, James 51, 79-80, John 45, Mary 61
Heysett (Haysed) Henry 30, Joakim 38, John 29-31, 38, Lewis 24, 49, Margaret 27, 38, Robert 35, William 45
Highampton 13, 15, 29, 36, 38, 41, 47, 49, 95, 97, 112
Highweek 22, 31, 33, 47, 54, 102, 107-108
Hillmoor 47
Hillmount 115, 130, 139
Hitchings, Evan 93
Hobbs, Frederick 53, Maggie 68
Hockin, Abraham 45, 57, Elizabeth and Richard 58, Henry 57, William 56-57
Hole 18, 49, 51, 99, 107-108, 111, 130
Holemoor 55, 98-99
Holland, William 38
Holsworthy Union 57
Holy Well 32, 136
Home Farm, Chilla 33
Homeleigh 130, 143
Hoop (Hope) 47, 97, 103, 105, 110, 112
Hooper, Cecil 131, Samuel 65, 131, William 55
Hopper, Benjamin 55, 99, John 47, 106-107, Oswald 129,
Hopton, Ralph 35-36
Horn, Emmanuel 45, 53, 61, 65-67, Mary 139, William 49, 139
Horrell, John 40, 49, Mary & Nellie 96
Hozer 19
Hundred of Black Torrington 14, 18
Hunkin, Edmund 45, Harold 69, James & Robert 97, John 97, 99, Jonas 43, 97, Nellie 102, 145, Ralph 43, 120, Samuel 43, 45, 47, 49, 139, William 54
Hunt, Arthur 93
Hurst 18
Hutchings, Bethuel 55, Daniel 99, Fanny 58, 100, John 49, Richard 107, Samuel 53, William 99
Hynes, Mervyn 131, Mrs 116, 130, 136

I
Isaac, Arscott 54-55, 112, 115, John 53, 100, 107, 112, 116-118, 129, 141, Lewis 53, Michael 110, 119, Susan 43, Walter 129, William 43, 47, 69, 103, 106, 130
Ivey, Alice 75, Fernley 121, 123, John 70, Leslie 10, 121, Michael 92, Thomas 130, 141, William 75-76, 120, 123, 135
Ivy House School 72

J

Jeffery, Nicholas 45, Thomas 25
Jenn, Charles 103, 106
Jennings 31
Jewell, Lizzie & Mary 96
John (King) 19
Johns, Courtney 92, Francis and Joseph 45, James 49, John 47, William 115
Jones, Alan 119, Arthur 130, Esther, Ken & Lorna 70, William G. 66, 104, 106
Jourdan, Mrs 113
Jury, Alfred 69, John 43, 47, 54-55, 93, 106-107, 109, 132, 136, Mary & Rachel 70, Rhoda 90, Samuel 45

K

Karinya 63
Keast, Audrey 69, Jean 127
Kelly, Beryl 91, Edred 54, John 47, 53-54
Kelly's Meadow 108, 115, 121
Kenneland 15, 19, 30-31
Keyethern 19
Keynes(Keines) 18, 23
Kilgannon, nurse 141
Kinge, Humphrey 35, John 29, 31
Kingsley 45, 50, 103-104, 130, 136, 141
Kingsmoor 18, 45, 57, 133, 147
Kite, Samuel 75-76
Kite Cottage 75
Kivell, Bernice 135, Colin 110, 121, 123, Freda 145, Graham 119, Heather 92
Kneela 18, 33, 41, 43, 104, 108
Knight, Elizabeth 70, James 77, 99, 110-111, 142, Jessie 96, John 49, Queenie 113

L

Lake (Shebbear) 97
Lake, Bampfyld and Elizabeth 37, James 37-38
Lamble, Robert and William 75-76
Lana 47, 54
Lane, Faithful and James 45
Langman, Ann & Bill 70
Larches, The 49, 51, 55, 59, 61-64, 104, 106, 123, 132, 145
Lashbrook 15
Lavers, Barraud & Westlake 82
Leach, Elias 25, 47, 79-80, Ezekiel 25, Richard 47
Letheren, William 47, 53
Lewis, Isaac 45
Ley 18, 35, 38, 75-76, 102
Ley, Desmond 70, Phyllis 70, 119
Limmbear, John 32
Llewellyn, Llewellyn 44, 53
Lock, Barbara 92, 114, Christopher 120
London House 139
Long Cross 32, 43, 55, 90, 104, 108-110, 136, 138, 141, 147
Long Hall 29, 33, 47, 54, 61, 72, 121, 125, 131, 139, 143
Lovies 31, 34-36, 41
Lucy, Geoffrey de 17, 19
Luxton, Archie 69, Ernest 11, 119, Fay 70, James 45, 99, Laura 11, 59, 116, Peter 120, Richard 99, Roy 69, Ruth 107, 114, 125, Thomas 66, Walter 142, William 121, 123

M

Madge, John 58
Mallet, Nicholas and Thomas 35
Malsters Cottage 143
Maltsters Hill 113, 139
Marland 17, 19
Marsh, Grace 47, Henry 45, Samuel 118, Thomas 42, 45
Martin, Cecil 143, Ernest 11, 122-123, Ethel 69, Frank & Raymond 70, George 54, Margaret 119, Nicholas 18, Stella 70, 145
Martyn, William 18
Maxwell, John 49
May, Barnabas 41, Samuel 45
Maynard, Clara and George 97
Maynard (nee Broad) Stella 11
Mayne, Joel de 17
Mearns, Lew 143
Methodists 97-98
Metters, John 97
Midelcota (Middlecot) 14, 15, 19, 45, 49, 103
Mill 19, 32-33, 45, 139
Millford, John 42
Millman, Alice 135, Gladys 137, Velma 92
Mills, Charlie 96, Emily & John 66, 96, Peter 63, Robert 66, 68, 72, 103-104
Milton Damerel 15, 65
Milverton, George 47
Mitchell, Caroline 68-69, 72, Henry 131
Moast, Bill 134, Cecil 69, 110, Florrie 102, John 106, 132
Moor View 141
Morgan, Allan 122, Arthur 133

N

Newcombe, Fred 143, William 102
North Devon Railway 107
North Devon Yeomanry 80
North Lew 38, 42-43, 88, 97, 99, 127-128
North Molton 17, 42
Northcot 15, 17, 54
Northcott John 91
Nucombe, Thomas 27

O

O'Bryan, William 97-98
Ogden, Tom 76-77
Oliver, John 30, 35, Richard 29, 31, 44, Robert 35, Thomas 29, 35
Osborn, Elizabeth and James 57
Ough, Brian 141, 143
Owen, John 61, Sir John 132, Willoughby 44, 59, 61

P

Pack Horse Inn 57-58
Paige, James 45, 79, John 30, 32, George 24, 41, 47, 49 Richard 79, Susanna 47, William 44
Park View 75, 141
Parsons, Amos 47, Joan 35, John 19, 29, 35, 69, Richard 41, 55, 141, Thomas 29-30, William 116, 143, 145
Passaford 81
Passmore, George 65
Payn, William 23
Peacock, Miss 51, 61
Pearce, Frederick 76-77
Pellews Cottages 20
Pellew, John 97, 103, 112
Penleaze, Alethea 81-82, Emily 81, John 24, 65, 81-82
Pennington, John & Thomas 43
Penwarden, Elizabeth and Samuel 65-66
Perkin(s), Fred 129, Humphrey 42, George 115, 121, 129, Joy 64, Lewis 103, 129
Perry, Arthur 141, 143
Peter, Apsley 54
Petherick, Arthur 45
Petrockstow 13, 17, 19, 79
Pett, Barbara 72
Phillips, Percy 141
Pierce, Courtenay 44
Piper, George 49
Pole, William 9, 17
Poltimore, Lord 81-82
Polwhele, Richard 9, 18
Pope, Hilda 106
Poplars, The 33, 103, 143
Porch House 65-66, 86
Potter, John 34
Powell, Revd. John 9, 33, 53, 82, 133
Prideaux, Zenobia 33
Priest, Gary 114
Prince of Wales 86
Protestation 34-35
Public Hall 56, 60, 70, 72, 104, 113, 115-120, 123, 130, 136-137

R
Reading Room 101, 115
Reed, Revd. Ford 98
Reedy Park 41
Reichel, Lucius 66, 86, 88-89, 102, Oswald 9
Residents' Association 147
Risdon, Anne 51, Edwin 53, 101, 112, Elizabeth 57, George 44, 47, 53, 93, 101, James 47, 54, 91, 101-102, 106, John 101, 113, Joseph 47, Susanna 101, Tristram 9
Robinson, Don 121
Rockey, Thomas 45
Rolle, Lord 49
Rose Cottage 41, 104, 136, 141
Rourke, James 73
Rowlands, nurse 141
Rudall, Robert 59, 61
Russell, John 82-86, 133, Percy 13

S
St Maur (Seymour) 22-23
Sadler, James 61
Sanders, John 25, 47, Robert 129
Saunders, James 45, W.A. 65
Schofield, Major 130
School House 66
Scott, Col Woodward 91
Scott Browne, Arthur 116,136
Seaward, Harry 79, 92
Shearer, Moira 124,127
Shebbear 16, 43, 51, 61, 97-99, 106, 112
Sheepwash 36, 41-42, 45, 47, 51, 59, 72, 80, 97-98, 100, 112, 130
Shoemakers Cottage, 141, 143-144
Short, J.S. 18
Shutt, Thomas 29
Silke, James 38
Sillifant, Fred 92, John 45, Trevor 70
Slade, Albert 120, 131, Bill 69, George 75, Maud 75-76, William 110
Slader, Agnes 30, Thomas 29
Slee, Charlie 116
Sleeman (nee Dart) 11
Sluggett, Beryl 121
Smale, Bernard & Derek 70, George & Humphrey 35, James 88-89, John 31, 34, 99, Nell 30, Robert, Susanna and Thomas 35
Smith, Jane 30, Jason & Jeremy 92, Marjorie 123, Pat & Mike 119
Smithsland 32, 91, 102, 104, 130, 146
Snow, R.M. & Co. 141
South Tetcott Hunt 127, 134, 136
South Trew 103, 112
Southcombe, Arthur 47
Sparke, James 44, 53, 72, 91, 102, 104, 106, William 102
Sparke Villas 73, 76, 101
Speake, John 18
Speccot's Charity 43, 102, 104, 107
Spencer, Edward 66
Spry, Shadrack 45
Squance, Richard 99
Squire, John 45,57
Stacey, Andrew 128, Shadrack and Thirza 58
Stanbury, Leslie 69, 72, 115-116
Stapledon, Bishop 23
Stenlake, Alice, Brian & Jean 70, Joan 42, John 44, 47, Nicholas 29, Richard 25, 44, 49
Stephens, Dorothy 72
Stettaford, Richard 79
Stevens, Thomas 27
Stidwell, Tom 133
Stores, The 104, 106-107, 112, 139-141, 143
Stucley, Sara 49
Sunday School 33, 81, 91, 99, 101
Swimbridge 82-83, 86

T
Tanton, James 47, 49, John 44
Tapley, Thomas 61
Tarring, Robert 75
Thomas, Freddie 141, 143, Maurice 11, William 92

Thorne, Nicholas 27
Tithe map 24-25, 47, 57, 97
Torintona (Torrington) 14-15
Torridge House 107, 139-141
Torridge Inn 60
Torridge, river, 12-13, 16, 53, 108, 116
Torrington, Great and Little 14
Totleigh 13, 15, 17, 19, 45, 49, 103
Totleigh Barton 16-17, 19, 49, 101
Town Meadow 108, 112, 146
Train, Jack 127
Trengove, Joan 72, 125
Trew 18, 47
Tucker, Anthony 44, 49, 79-80, 101, Eliza 101, Audrey & Shirley 119

U
Union Inn 47, 54-60, 75, 127, 133
Upcott 18, 49, 72, 109-110, 112, 139
Upcott Avenel 38, 51, 58

V
Vancouver, Charles 49
Vanstone, Ann 99, Arscott 141, Charity 47, Elizabeth 143, Isaac 53, 141, James 47, 103, 107, Mary 143, Samuel 45, Stephen 99
Veale, James 81, Westcott 44, 51, 81
Venn 14, 104
Venn Meadow 121
Venton, Arscott 25
Victoria Road 110, 113

W
Walter, John 49
Wanford 15, 17-19
Wanford (de), Eustace, Nicholas & Richard 18, Thomas 18-19
Ward, Miss A. 72, George 49, Henry 103, 106, 129, John 45, 98, Philip 129, Stephen 49
Ward Jackson, C 136, 141
Webb, Stephen 35
Weekpark 19, 43,
Westcote, Thomas 9, 15
West Devon Electricity Co 108
Westlake 99
Wheadon, Thomas 72, 132, 136
White, Agnes 29, Beatrice 72, Thomas 27
Whitelaw, Francis 72
Whiteleigh 15, 17-19, 23, 33, 49, 133
Whitlock's 116
Willis, David & Sheila 92, Sylvia 70, Tom 113
Windmilland 47, 107, 110, 112
Winser, Albert 70, 76, 121, 130, Dawn & Melina 70, Dolly & Kit 69, Percy 69, 131, Vera 92
Winsford Hospital 62-63
Wistaria 73, 82
Wivell, Annie 145, Dora 70, Samuel 107
Women's Institute 108, 116, 120, 123, 137
Wonnacott, George 45
Woodhills 56, 107, 113, 120, 130, 139
Woodley, Henry 139
Wooldridge, Benjamin 45, 49, Elizabeth 145, Emanuel 112, Jack 69, Bessie & Mary 96, William 98-99
Woollcombe, John 49
Worsley, Rachel 137, R. Carmichael 62
Worthe Moor 32

Y
Yelland, John 47, Priscilla 70, William 53, 99
Yolland, Anne 34
Yonge, Denys 44, Thomas 29
Yorland, Richard 29
Young, George Martyn 18
Young Tradesmen's Club 59
Yule, John 133

Z
Zouche, 17, 19, 22